NOW AN INVESTIGATION DISCOVERY TV SPECIAL

a

TASTE
for
MURDER

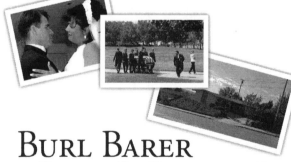

BURL BARER
& FRANK C. GIRARDOT JR

WILDBLUE
PRESS

WildBluePress.com

A TASTE FOR MURDER published by:
WILDBLUE PRESS
1153 Bergen Pkwy Ste I #114
Evergreen, Colorado 80439

WILDBLUE PRESS is registered at the U.S. Patent and Trademark Offices.

978-1-942266-35-8   Trade Paperback ISBN
978-1-942255-36-5   eBook ISBN

Cover Design and Interior Formatting by Elijah Toten
www.totencreative.com

Introduction
by Burl Barer

How do I kill thee? Let me count the ways.

Guns, knives, blunt objects, strangulation.

No matter who or how you slice or shoot, killing is a messy deal. Guns make too much noise. Bullets can be traced. Then there's the blood.

Anyone who reads true crime knows that all murders require motive, means, and opportunity. "Means" is the method of murder—the gun, the knife, the hammer to the head.

Sometimes the police conduct brilliant investigations leading to an arrest. Other times, the killer is an absolute idiot who does such things as leave MapQuest directions from their home to the crime scene. Today, with all the modern advancements in technology, we think cops can swoop in with a CSI team and solve anything.

That's on television. In real life, it's not that easy, and we've even had the head of a CSI lab sent to prison for faking evidence that put innocent people behind bars.

So, back to basics. Killing me loudly with your gun is not a good idea by any standard.

If the victim isn't holding one in his hand when the cops and coroner get there, they will figure out pretty quick that they are dealing with murder. And even if the dead body is clutching a hand gun, if the shot was fired from five feet away it proves that the killer failed an attempt to make it look like suicide.

Discussion about such matters are the stuff of conversations with crime writer Frank Girardot, Jr. at a Starbucks in Pasadena, California, not too far from the route of the annual Rose Parade. No doubt the other patrons find our cappuccino-laced detailing of death, dismemberment, manipulated crime scenes, and diabolical schemes either repellant or fascinating. In Pasadena, coffee shop conversations usually avoid such discomforting topics.

Frank knew a guy who did time in prison for a 1967 murder up in Fresno. The guy used a gun, and he threw the murder weapon into the Yosemite River. Well, almost. The cops found it on a cement pylon holding up a bridge at the Madera County line. He missed the river by less than a foot.

That guy was a pimp. And the victim was a customer down in Farmersville who got rough with one of the girls. In the pimp code it's the sort of crime that cries out for justice.

Doing time with guys like Jimmy "the Weasel" Fratianno, other big-time mobsters, second story men, flim-flam guys, and an assortment of jazz musicians popped for dope crimes in a less progressive time, Frank's pimp pal learned a lot about how cops, prosecutors, judges, juries, and straight citizens viewed gun crimes.

Shoot a guy once, you might get away with self-defense. Shoot him once in the back? Nope. At close range? Nope, that doesn't work either. Shoot him more than once, every bullet that enters the dead man's body exponentially lowers your chances of getting off.

Think a sharp knife might be better?

Probably not. You have to get up close and personal with a blade. Unless your victim is asleep you're going to have to fight to record the kill. Rest assured there will be a mess. Chances are you'll get hurt too.

Great example of that is the 2014 knife slayings of Pasadena chef Larry Bressler and his wife, Diane. The

Grateful Dead fans, who wouldn't harm a flea, were knifed to death in their apartment on North Madison Avenue.

The alleged killer got wounded in the attack. He was caught wandering the early morning streets of central Pasadena covered in blood. It is difficult to create a convincing explanation to the cops as to why you're covered in blood, especially when it isn't your own.

Spokane serial killer Robert Lee Yates, Jr. came home one night with the inside of the family van soaked in blood. He told his wife and kids that he hit a dog, and he took the dying, profusely bleeding animal to the pet hospital. They believed him until he was arrested for murdering at least eighteen women. Nothing like having a beloved family member arrested for multiple homicides to have you reevaluating their explanation for any event involving blood-soaked anything.

For the sake of discussion, let's say you kill two people with a knife. If you don't want to get caught, you not only have to get rid of the knife, but stabbing and slashing people causes extreme amounts of blood. And as you are right there when the blood spurts, you are going to be covered in it.

This was one of the many "reasonable doubts' that the jury acknowledged in their verdict of not guilty in the famed O.J. Simpson trial. After all, Ron Goldman was slashed and stabbed over twenty-two times. Nicole Brown's head was almost completely severed from her body. Over three pints of blood spurted from their bodies in a ten-by-ten enclosed area. The murderer would be completely drenched in blood, even more so than the man found wandering the streets of Pasadena.

The LAPD found no blood from the victims anywhere on anything related to Mr. Simpson other than the few spots which the expert from the FBI confirmed were from the sample Mr. Simpson provided police after he returned from

Chicago, after the murders. The LAPD even dismantled all the plumbing at Simpson's home and found no trace of blood in any of the pipes. None.

In that case, it was the significant lack of blood evidence, and the offensive alleged planting, for whatever reason, of a few spots by police, that gave the jury more than reasonable doubt.

Moral of the story—unless you are a trained Columbian drug cartel executioner with no known personal connection to your victims or you are someone with the psychiatric condition of "Violent Rage Disorder" with a history of attacking people with knives who was, immediately prior to the murders, stood up for dinner by Nicole Brown but somehow escaped serious consideration by law enforcement—knives are no way to commit murder.

How about you murder with your bare hands? That's called strangulation. That requires strength and about five minutes of stamina. Forensic experts can extract fingerprints from skin-to-skin contact, so you'll have to wear gloves. Unfortunately, gloves could leave fiber evidence behind. Strangle somebody you know, and the cops will have you confessing to it before twenty-four hours have passed.

Ligature strangulation isn't much better. Use a rope, a cord, a wire, and there's a great chance the cops will find the receipt from the hardware store where you bought the rope, the cord, or the wire. Oh yeah, it will have your credit card number on it too.

Oh, you paid cash? Don't think that will help. The kid behind the cash register will circle your face in the six-pack of mugs he's offered. And, guess what? You're going to jail and then prison, and it isn't anything like *Orange is the New Black*.

There's the old blunt force trauma route. Frank remembered a guy who killed his wife with a frying pan or a teapot or some other kind of kitchenware. The couple had been married for years, when the husband just snapped. Maybe he'd been nagged too much. Maybe she undercooked his steak or refused to clean his skid-marked undies. Who knows? He felt bad enough about the whole deal to stand around and wait for the cops to come and arrest his ass. He probably learned in state prison exactly how difficult it is to be someone's wife.

After blunt force, there aren't many options. You could go on a cruise and throw your spouse overboard at sea. You could hire someone to do the dirty work—that never pans out because most killers for hire are also cops who, if you are not organized crime paying big bucks for a well-orchestrated hit on a criminal rival, simply arrest you.

There was a guy in Tacoma, Washington, who murdered his wife and thought he could burn her body in the fireplace. Sorry. The chimney caught on fire from her burning fat, and he was overcome by the smoke and rescued by firefighters. He woke up in the hospital handcuffed to his hospital bed.

You could try killing someone and make it look like it was a burglary where the burglar bumped off the homeowner. You think you're clever? It's all been done before. Forensic expert Brent Turvey has written extensively on this scenario and conducts seminars for law enforcement on manipulated crime scenes.

What does that leave us?

Mail bombs? Those are too many variables, and mail bombers make the mistake of believing that the explosion will destroy evidence. Nope. Sorry. Among the debris of the horrific Alaska Mail Bomb Conspiracy case was a little piece purchased from Radio Shack by the bomb maker. The sales receipt was on file.

In another case, cops found the stamp blown off the package. It had the bomber's thumb print right in the middle, clear as day, guilty as charged.

There are still ways of killing devoid of guns, knives, bombs, strangulation, or hammers. In fact, there is a method of homicide that was so popular in the nineteenth century, that people were bumping off each other right and left—friends, family, parents, husbands, wives, children, and even strangers—because there was no way to get caught. Some did it for the perverse thrill of taking human life, others did it as an act of revenge for a slight or humiliation, real or imagined, but most did it because they believed that killing another human being, even their own flesh and blood, would bring them some sort of increased wealth or advancement in social status.

"And the great thing about this method," I tell Frank at Starbucks, "is that it can look exactly like natural causes—the number one killer of vegans in America."

"Really?"

"Sure. All things considered, vegans die of natural causes. They drop dead in the aisles of health food stores while listening to NPR."

The woman behind us, overhearing our conversation, almost choked on her red velvet cupcake. Frank knows the Heimlich maneuver. His charming coauthor admits he does not but acknowledges he did learn the Conversation Step in a ballroom dancing class.

What does this have to do with cold-blooded murder and the horrific case that takes up the rest of this book? Plenty.

You are going to read about a nice guy found dead on his bedroom floor by his beloved bride. He wasn't shot, stabbed, strangled, or bombed. And even though he wasn't a vegan, it looked like natural causes—except it wasn't. It was the cold, cruel murder of a kind, loving man who treasured his wife and stepdaughter with all his heart.

Frank Girardot, Jr. and I selected this story because it is a myriad of stories in one—a multi-generational drama of love, loss, perversity, greed, madness, and murder. Ultimately, there is an allegation of *another* homicide, years earlier, that is so shocking in its implications that we ask you, once you have finished the book, to write us a note and tell us whether or not you believe the allegation.

Oh, and as with all true crime books, this is a version of events recalled from memory and adapted from personal in-depth interviews with diverse individuals, information shared by law enforcement, attorneys, newspaper reporters, private detectives, insurance investigators, and experts in diverse fields whose insights offer keys to understanding how such a heinous crime can be committed.

Any errors of fact are unintentional, some names have been changed to protect privacy, and certain conversations or comments required emendation and speculative reconstruction for your ease of reading and comprehension. Much of the dialog is taken from secret recordings presented as evidence in the murder trial.

What begins as an epic mystery becomes something far more perverse, bizarre, and as hypnotically fascinating as a tragic roadside accident, but this death was no accident. It was a cold-blooded homicide committed by someone with a taste for murder.

Montebello
Saturday, September 9, 2000
3:05 a.m.

September 2000 was a busy month in the Los Angeles County homicide business. A total of eighty-five residents were shot, stabbed, beaten, or strangled in thirty days. When you're a graveyard-shift cop in the LA County suburb of Montebello, California, you get used to dead bodies. They don't call it the graveyard shift for nothing.

Officer Stephen Sharpe rolled on the "927 David"—a possible dead body—as soon as the call crackled over his police radio. He arrived within minutes at a lovely ranch-style home in an upscale neighborhood known for stunning views and well-kept lawns. He rang the bell and was met by Angie Rodriguez, her body in bed clothes, her face puffy from crying, and her teenage daughter tearfully clinging to her side. This was the woman who called 911 sobbing, "He's not breathing."

"Nothing looked too out of place. There hadn't been a fight," Sharpe recalled, "Angie's husband—she said his name was Frank—wearing only a T-shirt, was lying facedown on the bedroom floor. Angie wasn't positive her husband was dead, but I bent down and checked his vitals. He was definitely dead, and his skin was cold to the touch. There was blood coming from his nose that was soaking into the shag carpet. Blood had begun to pool under the skin around his knees too."

A paramedic came in and confirmed what Sharpe knew and Angie suspected. Frank Rodriguez was dead of natural causes. There was no need for a homicide investigation.

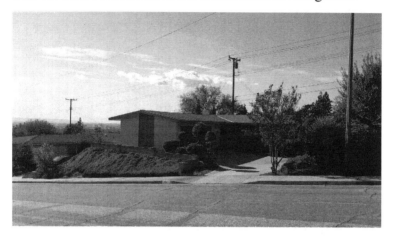

Montebello Police officers were called to this home in Suburban Los Angeles after Frank Rodriguez suddenly collapsed and died. (Photo by Frank C. Girardot, Jr.)

This wasn't the type of dead body Officer Sharpe most often encountered working the graveyard shift in Montebello—a shift aptly named for a sleepy bedroom community where six violent Latino street gangs lay claim to profitable turf. This case looked like a whole lot of nothing.

Frank lay on his belly. His legs were curled up in almost a fetal position. His face was puffy and bloated. There was a tiny pool of blood near his open mouth. His still eyes held a look of shock.

Sharpe called in Los Angeles Department of Coroner Investigator Brenda Shafer. As Shafer went to work examining all the particulars of Frank Hernandez's body, Officer Sharpe listened carefully to Angie's sob-punctuated synopsis of her dear husband's demise.

Angie's basic tale was this: On Tuesday, Frank returned from a field trip with the high school students he supervised at a school district boot camp. He felt "tired and groggy." Wednesday morning, he woke up, went to work for a couple of hours, but came home early not feeling well and looking flushed.

He began vomiting Wednesday night. By Thursday morning he was so ill he could barely move. Angie took Frank to the emergency room at Kaiser Hospital in Baldwin Park.

Frank's symptoms included extensive vomiting and three episodes of diarrhea. It looks like food poisoning or perhaps the flu, Dr. Chu told Frank and Angie. But just to be certain, Chu ran some standard lab tests.

The doctor wanted to measure Frank's kidney function in case he had stones. There was a sigh of relief when the blood work came back. It turned up nothing abnormal. Nothing out of the ordinary appeared in the tests. Chu told Frank he likely contracted a powerful strain of food poisoning. He instructed the patient to get plenty of rest and wrote in his orders that Frank was to drink Gatorade as a way to rehydrate his body. And with that Frank and Angie were on their way, hoping the illness wouldn't last much longer.

Angie picked up several bottles of Gatorade on the way back home, telling her daughter not to drink them because they were all for Frank.

When they got home from the hospital, Angie made Frank soup, and the family said prayers. The couple was demonstrably religious in both attitude and consistent behavior. Prayer was not a once a week or even once a day event—it was woven into the fabric of their lives and all aspects of their behavior were viewed in terms of the sacred.

They were truly the family that prayed together, in

sickness and in health. Angie, Frank, and Angie's daughter, Autumn, prayed that Frank would soon recover. Autumn loved her stepdad, and Frank doted on her. Eager to help anyway she could, the young girl brought him her mother's homemade soup, some tea, and more of the sports drink Frank enjoyed.

Even with the prayers, Frank's condition seemed to worsen as the night wore on. He was determined to shake it and be better in time to enjoy his family for the weekend.

Eventually Angie was so tired from the physical and emotional toll of taking care of Frank that she fell asleep on the couch. She woke up at 10:00 p.m. and checked on him one more time before returning to the living room couch and the final hour of primetime programming.

Law & Order: Special Victims Unit was on the tube. The episode focused on an attorney who was suspected of keeping a Romanian immigrant as a sex slave. Angie subreferenced her complete fascination with the episode to Officer Sharpe. At the end of the show's closing credits, Angie fell asleep.

"I woke up about three, and I said it's time for me to go to bed," Angie said to Officer Sharpe, "and that's when I found him. He probably got up to go to the bathroom and just collapsed. Or got up to do something and just collapsed."

Sharpe, who had been to dozens of similar scenes in his career as a police officer, retained his professionalism, taking copious notes and showing exceptional compassion, patience, and empathy.

"When you deal with someone such as Angie who has just had a loved one die, they are usually very upset and they don't want to talk to you," Sharpe explained. "The little information you get from them, it's hard to understand because they are crying, and they have a lump in their throat so to say. It is all very awkward, and it is very difficult to talk to them," Sharpe said. "You have to keep repeating yourself, and you have to really try to calm them down. You constantly tell them to take a deep breath and assure them that everything is going to be all right, and then, eventually you get a question in, and hopefully you get an answer"

It is difficult enough interviewing someone in shock, but when you add the emotional pain of sudden bereavement, you never really know how the person is going to respond. Angie was upset yet able to give Sharpe coherent answers and accurate information.

"As soon as I began speaking with her it was as if she forgot about what was going on. She would draw all her attention right to me and the questions I was asking."

There are, according to long-time investigative expert Fred Wolfson, individuals who process the first stages of grief by doing exactly what Angie did with Officer Sharpe. "By focusing on Sharpe and his questions, she could essentially tune-out the reality of her husband lying dead on the floor. The more she could focus on Sharpe, the less she would have to deal with the pain and trauma of Frank's death."

With Angie and her daughter in immediate need of spiritual strength, Pastor Joseph Garcia of the Pentecostal Word Aflame Church in nearby Whittier was summoned to offer comfort and condolences.

Word Aflame, one of thousands of such churches that operate out of old store fronts, ministers to recently arrived immigrants, the poor and middle-class devout souls such as Frank and Angie who come from a heritage favorably disposed to adult baptisms, speaking in tongues, and Frank's personal favorite, fire and brimstone preaching of intense emotional content.

Frank was a true believer of firm conviction whose faith was no new temporary fad or fascination but rather built on a solid rock of devotion in full force since his return from the Navy decades earlier.

When Garcia arrived at the Rodriguez home to comfort Angie, he reflected on his first meeting with the couple.

"When Frank and Angelina first came to our church," said Garcia, "they were very pleasant, open, and had the feeling like 'this is the place,' and we were immediately comfortable with them also. We all felt like we had known each other before."

As Garcia, Angie, and Autumn prayed, coroner's investigator Shafer rolled Frank's body over on his back. A mustard colored fluid was observed on the carpet. Taking out a post-mortem thermometer, Shafer jammed it into the body's core.

"Liver temperature was eighty degrees at 0538 hours. No obvious signs of trauma. Forty-one-year-old male ..." She needed Angie to answer a question and called out to her to come into the bedroom.

"What was your husband's full name again?"

Angie looked down at his dead body now rolled over on the carpet.

"Jose Francisco Rodriguez," said Angie, enunciating each syllable as if her precision in pronunciation was the deciding factor of Frank's destination in the afterlife.

"Did your husband want to be an organ donor, or do you wish to donate his organs?"

Angie stepped back as if the idea was somehow shocking. "No. No."

"Well, would you like to donate his corneas?"

"No, I can't see that happening," said Angie

The coroner's crew zippered Frank into a body bag and hauled him to their examination room on North Mission Road a few miles away. Sharpe, his partner Laura Flores, and the other Montebello officers left soon after, as did Pastor Garcia.

Frank's dead body was no longer on the bedroom floor.

He was not only dead, he was dead and gone. Angie's daughter, up with her mom since just after 3:00 a.m., had collapsed in tears and exhaustion following the prayers with Pastor Garcia.

Angie stood in the post death silence of her lovely ranch-style home in Montebello, California. She picked up the telephone and called her mother-in-law, Jean Baker.

The two women had never met. Mrs. Baker didn't live locally; Frank and Angie had a whirlwind courtship and were married less than a year ago.

"Frank's dead," said Angie. "He was sick, and he died."

Frank's mom was in shock when she heard the words.

"What did you say?"

"Frank's dead," Angie replied. "I'm sorry. He's been sick."[1]

When Frank's mother heard the horrible news, she immediately called Frank's younger sister Rebecca Perkins. Jean Baker was hysterical with grief, and Rebecca couldn't get much out of her because there wasn't much to get.

Upset and worried, Frank's sister called Angie herself to ask what had happened. It didn't make sense for Frank to be dead. He was never sick, he was always healthy, and he took great care of himself and had an iron constitution.

"He was more than careful about his health," insists Ms. Perkins, "Frank was fanatical about his health."

Rebecca Perkins desperately wanted to know what happened to her big brother, asking Angie, "What was the cause of death?"

Good question, but one for which Angie didn't have the answer.

In her traumatized and shocked condition, Angelina Rodriguez, whose husband was recently carried out in a

1. This conversation and many others in the book are transcribed directly from court documents and court testimony.

zippered black bag, looked at the supply of Gatorade recently purchased and mumbled a tragic non sequitur: "He drank too much."

Perkins was taken aback by the reply because alcoholism was a Rodriguez family curse.

"Our father was a drinker," explained Perkins, "and Frank had suffered his battles with the bottle, too. But I believed that Frank had kicked booze for good. Hearing Angie say that Frank drank too much made my heart sink."

Perkins wept into the phone, tears streamed down her face, and she sobbed out words of disbelief.

Suddenly, Angie had to hang up. There was a call coming through on the other line that she needed to pick up.

"It's probably Frank's reserve unit calling," she told Perkins. "They will want to know why he's not in today. I'll have to tell them he's dead."

"This is so tragic," cried Perkins. "Everyone loved Frank so much."

"Not everyone, Rebecca. Jesus knows we did, but ..."

The two bereaved women sobbed, but the conversation concerned Perkins. Who didn't love Frank? Almost as soon as she hung up with Angie, Perkins was on the phone with Sharpe, the first officer on scene earlier in the morning.

After talking to the cop, Rebecca called her sister Shirley Coers back in Central Illinois. Shirley, in turn, called Angie. Shirley had never met Angie either, but over the course of the next several days the pair had many telephone conversations about Frank's funeral arrangements. With that resolved, Angie turned her attention to what was, for her, the most important matter of all: why was Frank dead? She had to know, for her own peace of mind, the cause of death.

Hoping for an answer, she called the Montebello Police Department. Sgt. Greg Wilsey took the call.

"The doctor who examined Frank can't figure out exactly

how he died," Wilsey said. "It might be weeks before a cause of death is finally determined."

"I really need to know how my husband died," pleaded Angie. "It is important to me to know why he's gone. Can you understand that?"

"Angie, I really want to help you, and I understand you're going through some rough times. I know his doctor said it was some kind of food poisoning, but the coroner is admittedly having difficulty being more precise."

"Maybe he accidentally ingested something that he was deathly allergic to. God only knows, but I need to know," said the bereaved Mrs. Rodriguez.

"Well, I'll tell you what. How about if I send over a couple officers to check out if there is anything weird lying around the house?"

Angie agreed that was a good idea. She wanted this put to rest.

Jean Baker, Shirley Coers, and Rebecca Perkins arrived into town in time for the memorial service honoring Frank's life. The first thing they noticed about Angie was the first thing everybody notices. Be she happy or sad, bereaved or elated, Angelina's demeanor doesn't much alter.

"It's as if she's missing the depth-of-emotion chip," commented a former coworker. "She can laugh and she can cry, but neither one very intently or for very long."

Riding with her grieving daughter-in-law in a limousine after the service, Jean asked about the pretty pink and white flowers that grew along the roadside leading up to the cemetery.

"That's oleander," Angie explained. "It grows all over California. Real pretty but you can't have pets around it."

True. One dry oleander leaf is enough to kill your family dog. Unlike chocolate which is deadly to dogs but yummy to humans, oleander is so deadly to both pets and humans that it can't be burned as yard waste without risk of death.

If you're dead, you don't worry about such things. Frank stopped worrying about everything when he gasped his last, facedown on the bedroom carpet. After a short ride in a black zippered bag, Frank Rodriguez wound up on a stainless steel shelf a few blocks away from Montebello on North Mission Road in Los Angeles.

Frank Rodriguez's body would soon be taken off the shelf, further examined, sliced, opened, and analyzed in order to answer one all-important question:

"Why is Frank dead?"

Frank, who had been in the military was buried with full honors at Arlington Cemetery in Riverside, Calif. (Courtesy Photo)

A Closer Look

They say there's a million ways to die, but in reality death comes in just four forms.

It can be an accident. Say your girlfriend gets run over by a car. She dies. A coroner or medical investigator will term the death as an accident. In that case, the cause will often be the result of what scientists call blunt force trauma. We might say her skull was crushed or her ribs were broken and punctured her lungs and heart. But at the end of the day, the event may be an accident, but the method was blunt force trauma.

The second form of death is suicide. Say your boss jumps off the balcony of his Las Vegas hotel after losing a few grand at the casino. The ruling will be suicide. It was caused by blunt force trauma suffered in the fall.

Third, we have murder. Let's say the shop owner down the street forgot to pay his bookie or his dope connection. When the aggrieved collector comes around with a baseball bat he might get carried away and crush the skull of said shop owner. That's known as death at the hands of another. In Latin it's called homicide. That's the mode. But the method? Once again it's blunt force trauma.

Finally, there's natural causes. I think most of us agree it's best to go in your sleep. That's natural right? So is a heart attack. So is suffering with cancer for months or even years. Natural deaths can be detected. Usually the decedent has been in the care of a doctor familiar with his or her condition. Often times the dead man or woman expires in a hospice or extended care environment.

If a coroner even gets the case—highly unlikely in a natural death that occurs in the hospital—there is little doubt the mode will be listed as natural. And the cause will likely be listed as some medical mumbo jumbo that means nothing to anyone other than doctors and insurance adjusters and maybe the guy at a desk in a well-lit back office somewhere who is compiling actuarial tables.

Built sometime during the Cold War, the offices of the Los Angeles County Department of Coroner on North Mission Road, about two miles northeast of downtown Los Angeles, have all the warmth of the era. At the main entrance, double glass doors emblazoned with the block gold print favored by Los Angeles County announce this is the Coroner. Push the doors open and you enter a waiting room that hasn't been refurnished or refinished since at least 1975. It has been the final destination for thousands of Angelenos since it was erected in the mid-1970s during the era Thomas Noguchi, infamous "Coroner to the Stars," held weekly press conferences on The Manson Family slayings, the Hillside Strangler, or the latest dead celebrity.

The walls are wood paneled. An old-style office directory—a black felt board with white lettering—hangs between two elevators that have clearly seen better days. There are a couple of tables and maybe a magazine or two for folks who want to hang out and wait.

Fluorescent lighting gives the place its clinical feel.

To the left of the entry door there is a window—not unlike a teller's window at a bank in a bad part of town. A pass-through slot sits there for next-of-kin to get necessary paperwork, pick up property, and figure out when they can send the mortuary down to pick up the body of their recently departed loved one.

No one minds the window. Often family members have to push a buzzer and wait for someone to come up. They can read the magazines or attempt to decipher the graffiti carved into the paneling while they wait.

Outside the double doors and across a cement walkway lies another set of double doors. Inside are files and paperwork. You can buy a copy of an autopsy report here. Many times insurance companies will require one before they approve a payout.

Even though it appears as if the two buildings are separate, they are connected. A long and low-slung rectangular stucco building bridges the gap. Past the second set of double doors is a loading dock. Frank's body was delivered the same way thousands of others have been brought down.

Autopsies are done on the second floor of the complex. Bodies are typically wrapped in plastic, stacked in a refrigerator and wheeled out on gurneys when it's time to be examined. The process itself is gruesome. Organs, including the brain, are removed. They are examined and weighed. Pieces of liver, kidney, and brain are saved for toxicology tests that require a variety of techniques, which include turning a piece of one's liver into a slurry of sorts that can be run through an centrifuge in test tubes that have been cleansed in an autoclave to assure the certainty of results.

There's a room in one section of that back building where scientists keep brains. The organs are placed in a nylon net and lowered into a formalin solution to prevent their decay. Often they are examined and studied for signs of Alzheimer's or stroke. After a while you can tell a lot about a human's condition by examining his or her naked brain.

There are other rooms where scientists keep all sorts of specimens. In one room devoted to tool mark analysis, the skeletons and skulls of murder victims tell awful tales.

One skull, for example, has two perfect rectangular holes at its crown. Look closely and you'll see the holes match those on the back of a claw hammer. Do the math and you can pretty much guess that whoever inhabited that head took a hammer blow and died as a result.

Another skull bears the tiny cross hatch left behind after it was stabbed with a Phillips screwdriver. A third has been caved in with the end of a pistol. A fourth lies in pieces partially crushed by a curved object like a baseball bat and partially crumbled when it was run over by a backhoe during excavation.

Elsewhere sternum and rib bones show off the fatal nicks they received from knives, saws, swords, and other sharp objects.

After a brief visit one learns that that there are a whole host of tools that can kill and kill effectively. It's always up to the coroner—or his criminalist—to figure that part out.

Brenda Shafer was suspicious about Frank's death from the moment she arrived.

"My job, when I go out on the scene, is to interview all witnesses," explained Shafer. "I collect any medical evidence I can find and have a look at the body to see if I can see any outward signs of trauma or anything that will give me an idea about what happened."

After conducting her investigation, Shafer noted that there was nothing in the house indicating either suicide or an accident. "He had no history of drug use. It didn't look like he fell," recalled Shafer, "and there were no obvious signs of trauma."

Shafer's most important comment in her official report was on the first page. She labeled the suspected cause of death as "Natural/Homicide."

Shafer wasn't the only one who found Frank's death suspicious. "Officer Sharpe stated that he notified his department of the suspicious circumstances, but detectives declined to respond to the scene at this time," recalled Shafer.

If someone had it in for Frank, an investigation was called for. As for the suspicious circumstances, they were simply this: there was no known reason for Frank Rodriguez to suddenly die. The man was one hundred percent healthy except for the fact he was also one hundred percent dead.

Healthy people seldom drop dead. Hence, a complete autopsy to examine all his bodily organs and brain was performed. As much as Angie wanted to know why Frank died, the medical examiner wanted to know even more.

Dr. Ogbonna Chinwah, a Los Angeles County medical examiner, performed the autopsy at 9:00 a.m. on September 9, 2000.

"At the time I began the incision into Frank's chest, I had performed about 4,000 autopsies," said Chinwah, a graduate of Loma Linda medical school who did his residency in pathology at the University of Southern California, became a certified pathologist, and after participating in a fellowship with the Department of Coroner, earned his certification in forensic pathology.

When asked to define his work, Chinwah gave this succinct reply: "My job is to determine the cause and manner of death in human beings. Typically, the process takes anywhere from twenty-four to forty-eight hours. Generally, we do it in the same day, but occasionally there are some cases we do it the following day."

Frank's autopsy, and the determination of cause of death, did not take twenty-four to forty-eight hours. It took a hell of a lot longer. What began as a normal procedure to determine cause of death turned into a baffling all-consuming medical mystery.

On TV shows such as *CSI* or the classic series *Quincy*, the mystery is solved before the final commercial. Frank's death did not pause for commercials, and the truth behind this man's death proved incredibly illusive.

Frank's eyes showed no signs of the hemorrhages that are common in victims of strangulation or suffocation. His nose was clear too. Frank had all of his teeth. There were no marks on his neck. Frank's arms and legs, fingers and toes were neither deformed nor exhibiting any signs that Frank might be a secret junkie. There were no needle marks between his toes, no track marks on his arms.

The doctor cut Frank open and first checked Frank's throat. No ham sandwich caught in the thorax, no signs of trauma to the tongue. He didn't choke to death.

The area inside Frank's chest also appeared to be in fine shape. There were no signs of infection of the sort caused by a ruptured intestine or appendix. Similarly, Frank's heart was in fine condition.

He next examined Frank's digestive system.

"The esophagus is intact. The stomach is not distended by gas. It contains 50 cc of brown cloudy fluid ... portions of tablets and capsules cannot be discerned in the stomach."

As he continued on with the examination, Chinwah found Frank's liver, spleen, and gall bladder to be "unremarkable." Frank's kidneys were normal. Frank's bladder was distended and contained about a cup of "clear urine." He didn't appear to be a diabetic.

After taking a look at Frank's brain, Chinwah could only note there was nothing wrong with it either. He took samples.

"Representative sections from various organs are preserved in storage jars in 10% formalin," he wrote. "Sections of heart, lungs, kidney, and brain are submitted for slides."

Chinwah ordered up some photos and some X-rays, then sewed Frank back together.

The experienced forensic pathologist with over 4,000

autopsies to his credit could not find any anatomical reason why this man died. If there is no anatomical causes of death, the cause is usually drug related.

"The testing is routine," noted Dan Anderson, a supervising criminalist with the county coroner's office at the time of Frank's demise. "We did the common battery of tests and tried to exclude all the drugs of abuse," he said. "We were having to go through all these different types of tests just to prove what actually killed him."

"You think you can put blood in a test tube and say 'tell me what's in it,' but that's not how it works," said Shafer. "The first tests came back positive for promethazine and other antihistamines, which was anticipated, but no cocaine, no stimulants, no heroin, no methadone, no marijuana, or other drugs were present."

Acting on a hunch, a coroner's team went back to Angie's house in hopes of turning up something. They found some ant poison and other insecticides. Frank's blood was tested again. The results were negative.

This death was becoming an endless source of frustration and suspicion. No one dies without cause. Frank Rodriguez was too healthy to die, and without a cause, the coroner couldn't issue a death certificate.

Frank, a prudent and responsible man, had life insurance with his beloved wife as beneficiary. Without a death certificate, however, the insurance company couldn't settle the claim.

"As soon as the medical examiner provides a death certificate, Mrs. Rodriguez," the claims agent told Angie, "we will promptly send you a check. As much as we sympathize with your financial situation, we can't do a thing until we have the death certificate."

Her financial situation was dismal simply because Frank's paycheck stopped when his heart did likewise. This is precisely why couples buy life insurance, and Frank was, above all, a caring husband who lovingly made sure that his wife would be taken care of in case something happened to him.

Angie and Frank took out the policy in July, just after moving to Montebello. They found agent Mickey Marracino through an advertising insert in the local newspaper. Almost as soon as he got the inquiry, Marracino set up an appointment.

A onetime newspaper reporter, Marracino has a special ability to connect with people and is highly perceptive. Like all good salesmen, he notices the make and model of cars in the driveway and whether or not the Christmas lights are still hung from the eaves in July.

"There was nothing parked out front the day I met them," Marracino recalled. "That meant no early tip off to their sense of style or how they wished to be perceived by others. You can tell a lot about someone by what they drive. Except in this case I didn't have the information that puts my mind's wheels turning, anticipating certain personality types based on their choice of vehicles. The house itself couldn't tell me much. It was typical tract home in a typical neighborhood."

What the insurance man discovered once inside, however, was a couple whose dynamic was far from typical.

"It was Frank who came to the door," said Marracino. "He was a thin wiry guy with one heck of a powerful grip. I thought he was going to break my hand. Frank was a very strong presence."

In-home sales require a certain amount of script. The salesman, intent on closing a deal, wants husband and wife together. He knows that important family decisions require the couple to be of like mind, with their purposes harmonized. After all, both husband and wife have to sign on the dotted line.

"Now, a good professional salesman," the experienced agent explained, "understands that even though you are in someone else's home, you still have to establish yourself as the one in control of the situation and the presentation. Sometimes you can do that by simply asking for a glass of water. By the time the water is served, you have already seated yourself in a dominant position."

Another trick of the trade is getting the couple into their kitchen or dining room and sitting at the head of the table. That move is partially about dominance, but it's also about getting both the man and woman in a position where they are face-to-face with the salesman.

Marracino's well established and time-proven game plan evaporated the minute Frank delivered a wince-inducing handshake.

"Frank took immediate control and began telling me exactly how the meeting should be arranged."

"We were walking to the dining area, and he ordered me to sit in this one particular chair," Marracino said. "Usually I take control, that way I can face both of them at one time. See you don't want to have your back turned to someone, it's rude and they will instantly be turned off. It's better to face both. But Frank was in control. I did what he told me to do. I wasn't about to start off on the wrong foot."

Angie also sat down where Frank wanted her to sit, and Marracino took his standard mental notes on the personal characteristics of his potential clients.

"At first, she struck me as the essence of 'average.' She wasn't thin, and she wasn't overweight. She didn't dress in a manner that would, shall we say, highlight her charms or accentuate her attributes. Like I said, 'at first.' My appraisal of Angelina underwent significant alteration during that first meeting. I began with my usual warm-up about the importance of owning life insurance, and usually the couple is sort of settling in and listening to something that is basically one-two-three agree with me material. Nothing I say is intended to trigger any response except perhaps a head nod or an occasional uh-huh."

The agent's opening monolog was suddenly interrupted by Angie who unnecessarily and enthusiastically made his preparatory remarks all about her.

"I've experienced the deaths of people who were close to me," she announced as if testifying in church and gave the same pregnant pause as one does when awaiting an "Amen."

"Oh," responded the insurance man, not quite sure if she intended to follow up her statement with further painful details or was concealing the deceaseds' identities under a silent blanket of unpleasant memories.

Angie referenced a tragic episode from a previous marriage—the sudden crib death of her second child. "It sure was a good thing that we had life insurance on her," said Angie. With that tragedy put on the table, Marracino returned to his rehearsed pitch.

"Frank had an existing insurance policy through the school district and another through the National Guard, but the total of the two policies was insufficient to cover the mortgage, let alone allow for a widow to get back on her feet. I could see that and so could Angie. It became obvious to me as my presentation continued that Angie knew as much about life insurance as I did. She later told me that she formerly sold insurance for Prudential."

Frank agreed he would be covered for $250,000. When he took his physical, Frank passed with flying colors. It was agreed that Angie's teenage daughter would be the second beneficiary.

"With life insurance, the price, it's based on age and health status," explained the affable agent. "Frank got the best price. A smoker pays more than a nonsmoker, like that.

He was in perfect health, and the result was he got the best policy out there."

Marracino joked with the couple. He told Frank he knew he was a teacher from the moment he walked through the door.

"Oh yeah? How so?"

"You had a seating chart," Marracino said. "Only teachers do that."

Once the policy was in force, Marracino didn't hear from Frank or Angie until the day Frank's body was removed from the bedroom floor. There was a monotone message from Angie on his business voicemail.

"I have some bad news. My husband has died," Angie said.

Marracino called back later that morning and promised to expedite the process on his end. He said it could take seven to ten days to get a check but he would do whatever it took.

"How did he die?" Marracino asked.

"We don't know," Angie said. "That's the big question. He was such a healthy guy. The coroner is going to conduct an autopsy and find out."

"I'll call the home office and let them know we have a death claim," Marracino replied. "I'll help you fill it out."

"How long do you think it will take to process the claim?" Angie asked.

Marracino assured her that she was dealing with reputable people.

"This is a real good company," Marracino said. "They get high ratings for their excellent service. If everything checks out, you will get paid in seven to ten days. If there's a problem, I'll fight for you."

Angie was a grieving widow with bills to pay. As the policy's sole beneficiary she stood to get $250,000 cash. Besides, the premiums were up to date and Frank was a healthy man before his death.

"He was also a prudent, practical fellow," recalled the insurance agent. "Frank sincerely wanted to make sure that his wife and stepdaughter were taken care of if something happened to him."

Something happened to him, but Angie couldn't be taken care of until it was figured out exactly what happened to Frank.

In truth, a hell of a lot happened to Frank, and every traumatic hour following her husband's sudden death, Angie became increasingly strident in her emotional assertions about Frank's untimely demise.

"My husband did not die because he was sick," insisted Angie, "my husband is dead because he was murdered."

Angie didn't just mutter her allegations under her breath. She voiced her suspicions with increasing frequency and insistence every day for two weeks, then culminating in a barrage of accusatory telephone calls answered first by Police Sgt. Greg Wilsey.

"Listen to me," pleaded Angie. "There is something horribly wrong. There is no reason for my husband to be dead. I'm sure that he was murdered."

Part of some people's coping mechanism in the face of bereavement, especially when they are the person taking care of the person who suddenly dies, is to blame themselves. To deflect that unrealistic feeling of guilt, they will often shift the nonexistent blame to someone else. To the seasoned ears of law enforcement, that's pretty much what it sounded like, but you can't just let allegations such as Angie's go unchecked.

Angel Gate

"If someone did something to Frank," insisted Angie, "it would have been done at Angel Gate."

"Angel Gate?"

"Yeah, Angel Gate—the boot camp for troubled kids. Frank blew the whistle on a sicko who was doing stuff to the kids. That guy is still there, and he hated Frank for exposing him, and I don't mean exposing him the way the guy was exposing himself."

"Angie," asked Wilsey, "had Frank been back up at Angel Gate before he got sick and died?"

"Hell, yes," said Angie, "that's what I'm trying to tell you. I went over his travel schedule for the week prior to his death. And Frank had gone to Angel Gate Academy to chaperone disadvantaged youths who were going there."

"Really?"

"Listen, I believe Frank was murdered. His death wasn't natural, and it wasn't an accident. If you're going to investigate a homicide—and I mean the death of Frank Rodriguez—the place to start is Angel Gate."

Angel Gate Academy, formerly located 195 miles north of Los Angeles at a real National Guard Base, was where at-risk kids were subjected to a boot camp experience in hopes of turning them around and changing their lives.

"Teachers and parents hoped a month of physical activity and humiliation would turn these kids into model citizens," commented famed private investigator Fred Wolfson. "Sometimes the routine worked. Most times it didn't."

In fairness to Angel Gate, it managed to keep its name out of the gut-wrenching horror stories associated with similar teen boot camps in California.

Jasmine Velazquez, a Redondo Beach teen who was subjected to a horrifying youth boot camp experience in the nineties, said there was nothing fun and the only thing "uplifting" was when she collapsed doing push-ups.

"I had my hair yanked and had dirt kicked into my face, eyes, and mouth. If you fell," she explained, "you were kicked and pushed and yelled at. We were called fat, whores, stupid, bitches, maggots, etc."

Humiliation was a routine part of Jasmine's experience, and the dietary regimen included unique concepts of recycling.

"They tried to force me to eat my vomit," she recalled. "I couldn't keep anything in. Once, they hosed me after I threw up, had me roll around in the mud, and get in my sleeping bag like that."

Often the children were force-fed and forced to drink water beyond the capacity of their stomachs.

"We had that three times a day," she said. "That was the only time to drink. After, you would have to hold the canteen above your head and if any water dripped, you would have to refill the canteen and do it again. Most of the time, we just threw it up, and didn't get any water in our systems. One time, a sergeant yanked my head back, grabbed my canteen, and forced me to drink which made me gag. If you fell or were hurt, you were 'faking,' 'weak,' or 'lazy.'"

"The medic was not licensed. He watched a child have a seizure, and the staff yelled and kicked him for forty-five minutes. Then an ambulance took him away. They said he was faking."

31

Administrators also weren't above engaging in sexual humiliation.

"The 'medic' had me dance for him on [a] table, I was seventeen," Jasmine recalled. "If I didn't, he said the entire platoon would be punished by having to duck walk back up a trail we had just duck walked up. It hurt our backs, necks ... everything. I lost weight and was so bruised up. I also had a horrible cut on the inside of my thigh from not being able to change my pads."

The humiliation could be unbearable.

"They gave one teen laxatives, and made him put a tampon in his ass and hike like that. One teen, Espinoza, was overweight, and they would taunt her, telling her imagine there's a burger up that hill."

Angel Gate never had allegations of teens in attendance being shocked, water-boarded, beaten, threatened with knives, punched, kicked, and spit upon. Nonetheless, the Los Angeles Unified School District stopped sending kids to Angel Gate in 2005 after the Department of Defense cut off funding for the boot camp program. Interestingly, the department later provided the district with grenade launchers, Mine Resistant Ambush Protected Vehicles, and automatic weapons. Apparently inner-city educational priorities changed.

Before Angel Gate moved out of San Luis Obispo and to a new home in San Pedro, parents and administrators engaged in a debate about the merits of boot camp education.

Virgil Middle School teacher Theodora Beltson, who trained Angel Gate students on conflict resolution, insisted that Angel Gate gave youngsters a "fresh start."

"The kids are sometimes numbers," Beltson said.[2] "There,

2 From a Los Angeles Daily News story by Jennifer Radcliffe published Thursday April 7, 2005, and headlined: "LAUSD may close popular boot camp."

they have so much extra support. Soldiers, community college teachers, and LAUSD counselors all provided training and counseling for students at Angel Gate."

Angel Gate students confirmed that the program was tough, but unlike the hell-hole of Jasmine's experience, Angel Gate staff members were firm but compassionate, dedicated to the kids' well-being physically, emotionally, and scholastically.

"Some kids, they're doing really bad in school," said one graduate, "and once they go to Angel Gate, they will start changing their attitudes and life and start doing better."

If investigators were going to Angel Gate Academy, they wouldn't find beatings, bruises, and humiliation. They would, Angie insisted, find a sex-pervert with eyes for young thighs and a penchant for vengeance-driven homicide.

It wasn't only Angie's accusations that prompted investigative action. Frank's distraught family members also thought something was off-kilter, and the coroner's investigators still couldn't figure out why Frank was dead.

Montebello didn't have the budget or manpower for a full-blown homicide investigation, especially one of potential complexity and repeated long-distance travel, but the Los Angeles Sheriff's Homicide Division certainly did.

The first thing Monday morning, Montebello cops turned the strange case of Frank Rodriguez over to Sheriff Homicide Deputy Brian Steinwand and Sgt. Joe Holmes. Those two detectives, most familiar with busting homicidal gang members and drive-by shooters, set out to investigate the connection of Angel Gate Academy to the sudden death of a man everyone described as a natural born leader—Jose Francisco "Frank" Rodriguez.

While the shortest distance between two points is a straight line, the route Frank took from his home town of El

Paso, Texas, to the much beloved boot camp of Angel Gate Academy was far from direct and more than a bit torturous.

Route 66

Frank was born in El Paso, Texas, about seventy-two hours after Valentine's Day in 1959. He was the second of six kids and would emerge as a leader in just about everything he did.

Frank, (front row, far right) was the second oldest of six children. His siblings looked to him as a leader and steady influence in a sometimes unsteady household. (Courtesy Photo)

El Paso is a border town, and many of its residents, like Frank's father, have deep ties to Mexico.

In Mexico, Frank's father had been a doctor. But he crossed the border in search of opportunity and wound up as an orderly who was never able to pass his board exams. Frank's mom had been married once, she had a young daughter when she met "Paco," Frank's dad. The couple fell in love and married. Frank was their first child.

It would be years before Frank and his siblings had any stability resembling typical middle-class Americana, circa 1960s. El Paso, a rough and tumble town on the Rio Grande, can claim to be the home of Ft. Bliss, but it is also home to copper mines, oil wells, and sweat shops—a blue-collar town if there ever was one.

El Paso elected the first Mexican-American mayor in the United States in 1957, and by the start of the 1960s, El Paso was coming to grips with poverty, immigration, religious differences, and a growing sentiment that Mexican Americans deserved a place in the political conversation.

"Frank's dad didn't give a shit about any of that important social issue stuff," recalled an old family friend, "he just wanted to drink, fuck, and stay out of trouble"

Trouble avoidance meant packing up the family and moving, and it wasn't long after Frank's birth that the family pulled up stakes and scooted down to Mexico for a year or two. When the heat was off, Frank's dad brought the family north again.

Somehow they wound up in Maine. One or two winters in the frozen Northeast convinced Paco that he needed to find a warmer climate for his growing family. He took a job at the Lincoln State School in Lincoln, Illinois, founded in 1865 as "an Experimental School for the Instruction and Training of Idiots and Feeble-Minded Children."

One hundred years later, the school hired Paco as staff

doctor. No one on staff cared that his medical degree was not recognized in the USA. The patients, still considered idiots and feeble-minded, were not considered entitled to a degree of health care even remotely approaching that available to those who were not officially idiots

Perhaps idiocy is contagious, because Paco abandoned his family and stumbled off to Florida. Frank's mom was stuck raising her six children alone, and she did a remarkable job.

Frank grew up a normal child of the seventies. He was a sports fan and particularly a baseball fan. Living halfway between Chicago and St. Louis meant kids had to make a choice. The 1968 World Series, featuring the St. Louis Cardinals and the Detroit Tigers, cemented Frank's decision to be a St. Louis Cardinals fan. Although Cardinals pitcher Bob Gibson won three outings, it was the Tigers, behind the pitching of thirty-game winner Denny McLain and the tubby, but loveable Mickey Lolich, who took the series in seven games. It was a wonderful time to be a baseball fan.

On the other hand, Frank's younger brother chose to root for the Cubs, who nearly made the World Series in 1969 but instead suffered an historic late-season collapse. The two boys established a rivalry and often played games of hot box pretending to be players on their favorite teams.

As a teen, Frank listened to rock and roll. He cruised with his buddies on Woodlawn Road, once a part of the famed Route 66. On Saturdays the kids would hang out at the Schoolhouse, a burger stand.

Everyone loved big-hearted Frank. He was a peacemaker who just wanted to do good. In high school Frank played football for a couple of years. As a junior and senior he switched to wrestling.

"He was not a very big guy, but he was wiry and really enjoyed sports," his sister Shirley Coers recalled.

By the time he was eighteen, fresh out of Lincoln High School, Frank was married and enlisted in the Navy. Frank needed structure. Life at home with a single working mom and a handful of younger siblings that needed constant attention wasn't going to provide that. Joining the Navy did. As a sonar tech Frank cruised the world. He left small-town Middle America behind and visited far-flung ports from Japan to Alaska.

"He was married, but he would be gone for six months at a time," Frank's sister added. No young bride is one hundred percent comfortable not having a husband for six long months at a stretch. When Frank's two years were up, the Navy offered a bonus if he would reenlist. To his surprise, his young wife liked the idea, especially because they could relocate to San Diego

Frank agreed, and he soon was back at sea. Coming home when those two years were up, it was his wife who cut him adrift. The couple split up, but Frank decided to stay in California. He had grown to love the state, its climate, and its landscape. He told family members that he would figure out a way to pull himself together and set about looking for work.

"He was lost," said Coers. "He didn't know what to do when the split-up happened. I think the one thing Frank wanted was a family. He wasn't going to have that and felt like he had wasted several years going nowhere."

In San Diego, Frank started attending night school. For a time he went to work as a paralegal with an immigration lawyer. It was short-lived.

Next he took a job as a plumber's assistant. In truth there are plumbers that make more than attorneys, so, why not? Again Frank didn't last long. He drifted north from San Diego. Although he held an assortment of odd jobs, Frank began to realize his calling was the military. Since he'd already left active duty in the Navy, Frank decided to join the National Guard.

A National Guard buddy told Frank about a teaching gig overseeing wayward kids at Angel Gate Academy in San Luis Obispo. Frank eagerly took on the job and settled in on the Central Coast.

When he got to Angel Gate, it was like starting over. Frank had found his calling. He was over the heartache of his failed marriage and ready to start over. Frank's friends said Frank threw himself into the work. He dedicated himself to the kids and decided to work toward a degree of his own and a teaching credential.

The kids loved him, his colleagues loved him, and his family saw Frank's personality as the loving peacemaker slowly return. He wasn't lost anymore.

It was at Angel Gate that Frank met Angelina. She was everything he could ever want—undeniably attractive and completely committed to Jesus Christ as her personal savior. It was a match made in heaven. As to not allow mutual desire to impact their potential union, they promised to remain celibate until marriage.

To those who knew them, their mutual love and marital harmony seemed as assured and obvious as their shared Hispanic heritage. The heritage aspect, however, was an erroneous assumption. Angelina Rodriguez isn't Hispanic. Born Angelina Coliacovo, and raised in the Catholic Church, she is descended from a long line of Italian Americans who came to the USA in the 1890s.

"Oh, there is so much you don't know about Angie," remarked her longtime friend Suzie Pinkham.[3] "She was really good looking when younger, and she still has that

3 Suzie Pinkham is a composite character. The quotes attributed to Pinkham are derived from a variety of sources including court documents, psychological analysis, and newspaper articles.

femme fatale vibe. Smart? Hell, yes. Maybe a bit too sexually aggressive at times, but some men like that."

Smart, good looking, hardworking, and sexually proficient—that was the Angie Frank met at Angel Gate. "When it comes to sex," said Pinkham, "I don't know anyone who started younger, had it more often, or enjoyed it more than Angie. She gets what she wants because she has amazing determination. If she wants something, she finds a way to buy it; if she wants a man she seduces him. She is one resilient woman. Go ahead, ask her about growing up in the projects in Far Rockaway, Queens, New York. And while you're at it, ask her how many times she tried to kill herself before she was twelve."

Far Rockaway

Born in 1968, Angie spent her formative years on Beach Channel Drive in the Carleton Manor projects of Far Rockaway, Queens.

Angelina grew up in Far Rockaway Queens. An 11-story, 170 apartment project, Carleton Manor was a haven for drugs and gangs in the 1960s and 1970s. (Evidence Photo)

According to the New York City Housing Department, "Carleton Manor is an eleven-story building on the Rockaway peninsula in Queens featuring 170 apartments housing an estimated 402 residents. Rockaway Freeway and Beach Channel Drive surround the 3.33-acre complex. It was completed March 31, 1967."

Located on the far-west finger of Long Island, Rockaway Beach lies across Jamaica Bay from Brooklyn. Today, there's nothing glamorous or special about the place as it struggles to recover from the ravages of Hurricane Sandy. The tropical storm wreaked havoc on the northern Atlantic Coast in late October 2012.

Rockaway had weathered its share of bad weather, bad choices, and change since, in just a century, it was transformed from a small fishing village into summertime destination and then into a rough and tumble beachside ghetto.

Rockaway Beach was once a summer paradise for New York families seeking a break from oppressive city heat and August humidity.

"It was a wood-shingle paradise for my family. You see, we didn't have a house in Brooklyn, we lived in an apartment, so this was paradise for us," recalled a man whose family spent a decade of summers at the beach. "We had a back door that led to alleyways and courtyards for us to play tag and bingo and hide-and-seek ... we never stopped playing and running and being outside from dawn to dusk."

By the time Angie was born in the late 1960s, Rockaway Beach had gone into decline. And the neighborhood was well on its way to becoming ground zero for many of New York City's worst slums.

Rockaway Beach projects such as Carleton Manor, where Angie spent her youth, sprung from noble efforts in the 1950s to combat poverty. Why have so many vacant houses in the winter, when they can be lived in year-round? The city's housing authority sought to bring about a change in living conditions for many of its poorest residents. By clearing slums and moving the poor out of tenements and into apartments at the beach, city officials thought they could influence behavior.

Many of the city's criminals, disenfranchised, drug-addicted, or with co-occurring disorders gravitated to the projects like soup stains to a necktie. Rents were much cheaper, and soon the easily exploited among society's marginalized—the poor, especially those of darker skin— were living and dying in horrid squalor.

Down the street from where Angie lived, reporters uncovered a beach house where one hundred people survived in conditions beyond deplorable. Children played in close proximity to exposed electrical wiring where the only insulation was rat droppings and a thick layer of cockroaches. Each room came with the dwelling equivalent of moon roofs and minimal shared toilets where people learned the importance of immodesty and patience. Fire safety was encouraged by the lack of sprinklers, and secrecy was discouraged by line-of-sight holes in not only walls but also floors. Several children died of pneumonia due to lack of heat.

The response of city fathers was immediate and forceful. Lament the conditions and blame the victims.

"What else can you expect when you let ignorant Puerto Ricans and Southern-born Negroes move in? It's not just skin color, it's an entire slum culture that's part of their blood," asserted residents of other neighborhoods in words such as these while claiming significant insight into contemporary social problems. "No matter what building they move into, within twelve months it will be a slum—they bring the slum with them like an infectious disease. It's all they know, and you can't change them."

Although official corruption was rampant and anti- black and anti-Latino racism was pervasive, the community continued to transform.

By 1967 Beach Channel Road was lined with projects. Carleton Manor would be the last, the smallest, and home to Angie, her mother, and her older sister, Gigi. Angie's mom, Anita, was a nurse. She did her best to provide for the small family. She worked long hours and often wasn't home. Angie's dad wasn't around much either, except when he was sleeping off a binge. Sometimes he drove a cab. Sometimes he drove a truck. He earned the money he could and often blew it before providing for his wife and the two kids.

Anita remembered Angie as a rebel. She encouraged her daughter to attend school and behave, but Angie wasn't swayed. At nine she ran away from a babysitter and wound up in a city-run home for girls. Angie said she felt unwanted and didn't want to live at home anymore. Anita picked her up, listened to her complaints, dropped her off at school, and went back to work.

There's no other way to describe the Carleton Manor than simply calling it what it is: "low-income project housing."

The internet travel guide WikiVoyage.com warns that Carleton and five other Rockaway projects are some of the most dangerous areas in New York due to gang violence and the possibility of being caught in gang-battle cross fire. The same site also notes that assaults on tourists are rare because tourists rarely visit low-income housing projects known for gang violence.

The change that would overtake the housing projects was in the air when Anita decided to move her small family. To save money she gave up hiring babysitters and began leaving her daughters home alone. Soon, the family escaped Carleton Manor and moved into the bottom floor apartment of a Far Rockaway home owned by other members of Anita's family.

Anita would say later she always did the best she could for her children. She paid for Angie and her sister to attend St. Rita's Roman Catholic School through eighth grade. Although her sister would go on to attend a Catholic high school, Angie was having none of it. She attended Far

Rockaway High School instead.

Anita made it a point to attend weekly bingo night at St. Rita's and often left the girls in the care of their paternal grandfather who was a direct descendent of the branch of an Italian family that settled in Puerto Rico.

Grandpa enjoyed playing with his granddaughters and especially enjoyed masturbating on them. Perhaps that wasn't a common experience in your family, but sexual molestation was a regular and predictable event in the lives of his female grandchildren.

Monday night was bingo night for the ladies. Men stayed home and football and baseball games filled the fall and winter airwaves. During the off-season the networks offered "Movies of the Week." In the Coliacovo family, Monday night meant young girls getting together and watching TV at Grandpa's house.

The girls' grandfather would sit on the couch with all the girls sitting in front of him to watch television. The room would be dark except for the glow of the cathode ray tube. When he was "ready," dear old Gramps would clear his throat. If that didn't get the attention of one of the girls who knew what was up, he would rub the closest with his foot.

Angie's sister was the oldest, and he started with her. She said the first time it happened, he motioned for her to go to a back bedroom. "The girls all knew what to expect, and we all participated at one time or another. Sometimes he would have more than one of us at once, but usually only one at a time. Usually Grandpa would wait a few minutes, and then he would follow."

"I was eight years old the first time I was chosen," she said. "(Grandpa) told me to pull down my pants and lie on the bed. He then pulled his own pants down. He didn't get on top of me or anything, he would just stand next to the bed and rub his penis up and down."[4]

She found the episode confusing, but Grandpa seemed pleased and promised her a prize.

"Don't worry I love you. You're my best girl, you know. Don't tell anyone. We don't want them to get jealous. There will be a prize for you on the TV the next time that you come over."

It was only the beginning.

Angie's sister knew something was wrong with the situation. She didn't understand exactly what was transpiring or why her grandfather was exposing himself, but she intuitively discerned it was peculiar.

The girls voiced their concerns to Mom, but Mom ignored the protests. The next Monday night found the girls sitting back in front of Grandpa's TV waiting to see which of them he would take into the back room.

That second week grandfather initiated contact the same way with Angie's sister. He stripped down and rubbed himself on the young girl's stomach until he ejaculated. This new experience wasn't explained, but as he wiped her off, she was told it was "a mistake" and wouldn't happen again. Gramps even promised to give her two prizes, although he had never given her the prize from the previous week.

Gigi once again told her mother that she did not want to go stay with Grandpa on Monday night. When Anita said, "too bad," it set up Angie as Grandpa's new toy.

During the next visit, Gigi ignored Grandpa's request for playtime. Angie, however, not knowing exactly what sort of game Grandpa had in mind, was eager to play. She wanted the attention, and she wanted a prize.

When little Angie saw Grandpa masturbating, she had a strong suspicion that this was not typical grandfather/grandchild interaction. Perhaps more world-wise than her

4. Statement comes from testimony included in court documents.

elder sister, Angie was also braver. The second time that Grandpa took her in the back room she did her best to convince Gramps to take up another hobby. Instead, Gramps increased the diversity of the activities in his perverse playbook.

"If Grandma finds out about this," Angie warned him, "she'll kill you."

Grandpa laughed as if Grandma either knew it already or would never believe it. Angie decided to find out. When she told her grandmother what was happening, the woman listened carefully, even compassionately. A week later, Angie's grandmother died.

The burial of Grandma only delayed Grandpa's continued sexual interaction with little Angie. As the youngster's sexual proficiency and versatility increased, Grandpa's interest in the other grandchildren abated and he no longer masturbated. With a child as apparently compliant as Angie, he had no need to clear his throat or use foot signals to get sexual satisfaction.

Although Angie was seemingly enthusiastic about having sex with her grandfather, she wasn't convinced it was appropriate behavior. She voiced her concerns to her uncle, who said he would do something about it. A week or so later, the family buried her uncle.

Two people told, two people dead. Angie decided to take one final breach of confidentiality—she went to her cousin. Surprised, her cousin listened drop-jawed to the details, then dropped his pants so Angie could demonstrate the depth of her sexual knowledge.

Angie learned that saying no and asking other people to help her wasn't working. In fact, it was causing disaster. Perhaps fearing for her mother's health and life, Angie never discussed the molestations with her, and Angie's dad was not around enough to talk about anything.

The bingo nights ended about a year later when the family moved into another Far Rockaway apartment. An aunt lived upstairs, and she watched the girls. No more nights with Grandpa. Angie, however, wasn't done playing. No, not at all. Angie decided to milk Grandpa all she could, and Grandpa was happy to provide whatever material items Angie desired.

At some point, "She allowed it to happen," Gigi Colaiacovo said. "She was always looking to be accepted and looking to be 'Daddy's little girl.'"

While still in high school in Queens, Angie posed for a series of bathing suit photos that she kept for several years afterward. (Courtesy Photo)

The sexual relationship between Angie and her grandfather lasted longer than most American marriages. She and Grandpa got it on with intentional and unfettered frequency. It was no secret. They might as well have been displaying their inter-generational genitalia familiarity on the dining room table at Thanksgiving.

As he bought her fashionable clothes and gave Angie money whenever she asked, Grandpa continued to prey on the young girl, and she sank into a severe depression.

Angie would often walk alone through the Far Rockaway neighborhood and down to the shore. She would watch the waves roll in and wish they would take her away. She wanted to die. She wanted to be out of Long Island, out of New York for that matter, she wanted out of life

The first time Angie tried to kill herself was when she swallowed a handful of over-the-counter pain medications. All that happened was that she threw up. You can't blame Angie for the botched suicide attempt. After all, she was only eight years old.

The anguish and despair would come and go. Angie tried to cope, and she figured out a way to negotiate the nightmare of her life. As she became a young woman of high school age, she continued to dress in the fashionable clothes Grandpa provided and was knowledgeable enough about sex that she used it to get whatever she wanted from whomever she wanted it.

Psychologist Dr. William Vicary explained the psychology behind Angie's behavior.

"Many of the victims and the molesters will tell you this, many of the victims are lonely. They come from troubled families," said Vicary. "They crave acceptance, they crave affection, and this is what the abuser provides them. He manipulates them, he gives them gifts, he talks to them, he gives them what their parents are not giving them, and as the little kid, as sad as it is, and the FBI experts will confirm this, will trade sex for love. And so that's what Angelina was doing."

According to Vicary and other experts, the victims force themselves to believe that the molestation is in fact, affection. "In Angelina's case," said Vicary, "she was more interested in grandfather's attention and affection and the presents he would give her, so that when he was doing sexual things to her, she would actually pretend to be somebody else, this imaginary person called Victoria where she would kind of have a fantasy and go somewhere else while grandfather was having vaginal intercourse or sodomizing her."

Grandpa may have been into Angie in many ways, or every way possible, but the fact that Angie outwardly appeared to be okay with it made her the one to receive blame and family criticism.

Many families in which the situation is going on pretend as if everything is okay. When the child says something about being molested, they are accused of lying and are often punished for "making up" such accusations about a family member who loves them and has been so kind to them. This can also become a "blame the victim" situation where the child is blamed because she sat on his lap, kissed him, and hugged him.

The victims of sexual molestation suffer a loss of self-esteem and blame themselves for what was done to them. They say, "It's my fault. I must have done something wrong. There must be something wrong with me." And that's exactly the way Angelina came to think about herself, that she was defective, that she must be cursed, that she must have a sign on her that says, "Do things to me because I'm bad."

Life in the Far Rockaways was tough enough, and Grandpa's sick and foul manipulation of Angie made her depressed. She would often have deep fantasies about death and dying.

Victims of sex abuse are closely studied, and research indicates that one-third come through an experience like

Angelina's unscarred. These individuals are typically resilient and have support of extended families, friends, teachers, and religious figures and are able to work through the trauma. Another third are like Angelina's sister—traumatized and suffering from relationship issues. These are people who don't get into a lot of trouble with authorities but have problems in relationships.

The other third?

"These are the ones that probably are more traumatized over a longer period of time," explained Vicary, "and their lives wind up being very self-destructive and destructive. Suicide attempts, mental illness, criminal behavior, and in terms of many of the men who have been sexually abused, they turn around and become abusers themselves."

Studies done at the University of Southern California by professor John Briere found that the more severe the trauma, the higher the likelihood the victim will suffer permanent psychological damage.

In Angie's case the trauma was compounded by the fact her primary abuser was her grandfather. A person she should have been able to trust.

"This is a devastative betrayal of your trust, and it can be more damaging psychologically than actually being molested by a stranger," Vicary said. "It may also be more difficult to have family members believe that the abuse occurred. If you've been through these kind of experiences, lots of these victims are quite mixed up as to what is love and what is sex and who can you trust and who can't you trust, who is a bad person, so it causes a lot of trouble later in their dating relationships and in their marital relationships."

And so it was with Angie.

At age nineteen, Angie, attractive and well-dressed, was the neighborhood hottie and reputed punchboard. Seeking a change of pace, she married a kid named Hector Gonzalez.

In terms of relationship longevity, the marriage was a short one. It lasted less than a year.

Not quite 20 years old, Angie sought to escape an abusive family situation and a failed marriage by joining the United States Air Force. There she met her second husband. (Courtesy Photo)

"After the failed marriage," Angie herself said, "I started running ... running to find my place."[5] Running away landed Angie in Florida and enlisted for duty with the United States Air Force. Now blessed with a patriotic sense of service, and an extended family of fellow veterans, Angelina's life took an entirely new direction—one of structure, duty, and stability.

It was there that Angie fell in love with Tom Fuller, a good-looking, athletic Air Force cadet who captured her heart while knocking her up. Within three months, she was pregnant, married again, and joyous about the future.

5 From a Los Angeles Times story by Gina Piccalo published March 9, 2005, titled: "Fatal Lies."

Emergency Room

"My future with Frank," sobbed Angie, "was stolen from me. This was it. This was my last great love, and I'm not going to rest until the son of a bitch who murdered my husband is behind bars on death row!"

When Montebello cops finally took Angie seriously, they turned the investigation over to Los Angeles County, where Sheriff's deputies investigated fourteen homicides in and around Montebello and East Los Angeles in 2000. All the victims were males ranging in age from twelve to fifty-one.

Gang killings were the bread and butter of the county's homicide bureau, and the Montebello cops sometimes lent a hand rounding up witnesses or snitches. Within the Sheriff's Department it was frequently cops who worked with the street suppression units that were promoted to homicide because they understood the streets, the gang codes, and the intricate web of alliances and rivalries that defined LA neighborhoods.

Brian Steinwand was one of those. A young homicide investigator with the Los Angeles County Sheriff's Department, Steinwand came to the detail with ten years of experience as a street-gang investigator. He was partnered up with Sgt. Joe "Joe Bob" Holmes, a veteran homicide detective counting the days to retirement.

Steinwand's first case that summer involved the August 27 shooting death of a forty-eight-year-old Compton man identified as Larry Trinell Williams. The case came together easily. An arrest was made. Steinwand and Holmes celebrated their success.

There was the case of Mary Ella Shoupe to break up some of that monotony. Shoupe, fifty-seven, of El Segundo, was murdered by a serial criminal named Renal Wise. He was arrested based on a composite drawing made with the help of Shoupe's eleven-year-old granddaughter.

DNA evidence from a baseball cap linked him to the 1992 killings of the Alina Casteleiro and Nicole Paquette.

Rather than face trial and a likely imposition of the death penalty, Wise pleaded guilty to all three cases and got life in prison without the possibility of parole.

"He obviously committed some atrocious crimes that these relatives of the victims are going to live with for the rest of their lives," Deputy District Attorney Darrell S. Mavis told reporters in 2003.

Adding to the sort of doublespeak that fills blank space in the newspaper but means absolutely nothing, Mavis added he was happy.

"To be able to bring closure to this case at an early stage is extremely good for the victims."

Except the victims were dead.

Cops also had to deal with the drive-by shooting death of sixteen-year-old church choir member Amber Lasky. The young girl was shot to death as she stood outside her grandmother's home in the Athens district of South Central Los Angeles. Cops knew two things about her killer: he drove a white Mercedes and used an AK-47.

The man suspected in the slaying later killed himself in a gun battle with police officers hoping to arrest him for Amber's slaying.

Other cases that month included domestic violence, a dead hooker dumped outside an office building on North

Robertson Avenue in North Hollywood, a John Doe, and a couple of corner boys selling dope in the wrong neighborhood.

The death of Frank Rodriguez was something far out of the ordinary. A real change-of-pace case. The two detectives went to Montebello and chatted with the local investigators.

"We drove there and met with a couple of their investigators," Steinwand said. "They gave us a quick overview of what happened on September 9 when the victim died. Subsequently they called her in to come speak with us. We had just gotten the case. We knew very little about it. They just told us what she had told them to that point and what have you. That was about it. We then sat down in a room to interview her. They had a hidden camera and a microphone in the room. We requested that they audio and videotape it. This isn't strange. Anytime we are dealing with the death of a person that we do not know who did it—we were dealing with a spouse in this case—we have the opportunity to tape it ... and we will."

Like most buildings of its ilk, the Montebello police headquarters is a drab and cold cement building designed for a couple of utilitarian purposes. It's there as a base for the police and acts as the local lock-up for weekend drunks, wife beaters, and the occasional tagger.

Additionally, Montebello rents out a portion of its facility to the feds. It's a good place to hold high-powered gangsters like members of the Mongols or La Eme, when investigators want their targets out of the general population residing at the federal Metropolitan Correctional Center downtown.

The interview rooms are no better. Except for windows and one-way glass, the walls are bare. The setting is as clinical and unfriendly as one might imagine such a place to be. It's set up for videotaping and audiotaping of interviews.

Angie's first meeting of what would be several with detectives took place there. There was a bit of small talk before a standard line of questioning got underway.

Angie went through the history of her relationship with Frank, beginning with their first meeting in February 2000 at the Angel Gate Academy. She recited the basics—married in April and moved to Montebello to accommodate Frank's new job teaching underprivileged kids in the vast Los Angeles Unified School District. They moved to Montebello to shorten his commute.

Detectives asked Angie if she planned on staying in Los Angeles or perhaps heading back up the coast to San Louis Obispo—the lovely locale from which she moved prior to meeting Frank.

"I've got other plans," Angie answered. She mentioned New York and Paso Robles.

Getting down to business, detectives told her that the important thing was the timeline. They asked Angie to please, once again, detail Frank's movements in the days before he died. Angie laid it out clearly and sequentially, eager to cooperate fully.

She related how Frank left the house around 5:00 a.m. on Tuesday. He was off to meet a busload of kids at Adams Middle School near 32nd and Adams just south of Downtown LA. He got back home about 9:30 p.m.

Brian Steinwand asked if the group stopped to eat.

"They stop at the same Carl's Jr.," she replied.

"Between here and there?" Steinwand asked.

"San Luis," she answered. "He said he didn't eat lunch."

"He didn't eat?" Steinwand prodded. "And we're gonna get into that with what he may have ate, drank, and stuff like that, but in the meantime—so, he gets home Tuesday night, everything's fine. Did he tell you anything? What'd he tell you?"

"Well, first you know that I begged Frank to stay home and not go on that trip. He wanted to go for the money. He was the provider, and that's how Frank was. When he came home, I thought he would complain about how his coworkers were cold and wouldn't talk to him on the bus ride. I mean he'd come home every day stressin' over school. Okay? Shit you know, just nightmares. But he said, 'I obligated myself for them to go. You know I'll feel it—I'll feel it out when I get off the bus.'

"When he gets back I said, 'So how is everybody there?'"

Angie described his reaction as enthusiastic and elated.

"'They were great. They walked up to me, they hugged me, they, you know, said they missed me.'

"I thought it was unusual that they were being nice to him. But I didn't know the situation. I thought, well, maybe everything kind of settled."

By "everything," Angie meant the hard feelings about Frank outing someone at Angel Gate for sexual abuse of a child and others covered it up. That, she explained was a major source of tension and the supposed motive behind Frank's earlier unpleasant experience of someone apparently intentionally poisoning him with a spiked drink and some cookies.

Steinwand wanted more details about the drink and the cookies.

"Did he ever end up telling you who offered him that?"

She strongly suspected that Peter Robespierre,[6] one of Frank's coworkers at the Angel Gate Academy, poisoned her husband because Frank uncovered sordid details involving Robespierre's behavior with underage students at the academy. When Frank spoke up about it, Peter was more than miffed.

It was becoming increasingly clear that Angie was fixating on Peter's anger as motive for her husband's sudden death.

---

6 Not his real name.

"In the absence of certitude," explains famed private investigator Fred Wolfson, "people create their own certainty, based on whatever they find most comforting. Sometimes people become so attached to their self-made explanations that when the real one comes along, they have a hell of a hard time letting go of what their own imaginations have conceived. For this reason," elaborated Wolfson, "detectives were not about to take Angie's allegations as Gospel, Torah, Qur'an or even consensus-validated folklore—you don't buy-in simply because the bereaved is convinced, and Angie was hard selling that when Frank traveled up to Paso Robles as a chaperone, that's when Peter must have gotten to him."

Angie explained what happened the day after Frank returned from Paso Robles.

"He got up in the morning" said Angie, "He went to work, didn't say anything to me, and then two hours later he comes home. I said, 'What are you doing home?' He said, 'Well they didn't need me, and I'm still feeling kind of tired and drawn out, so I'm just gonna go lay down.'

"And he got up a couple of times, and you know, I had him drink some tea and—and, uh, I said, 'You know, make sure you drink a little water and, you know, maybe you're dehydrated, long trip, change of climates.' And, uh, then he says, 'You know, I kind of have a headache, and I kind of feel a little nauseous.' I'll just treat it like I would treat my daughter, you know, maybe she got a bug, and I kept checking his temperature. I gave him some soup, treated it like the flu, stomach flu, whatever. And then that night about 7:30, he started throwing up."

As Wednesday night wore on into Thursday morning, Frank's illness got a lot worse. Angie made an appointment for Frank at Kaiser in Montebello, but the facility couldn't handle a man as sick as Frank had become. By Thursday morning he could barely stand. The vomiting and diarrhea was striking every ten to twenty minutes. Angie took to cleaning the bathroom before they left for the hospital some fifteen minutes further away in Baldwin Park.

The emergency room was teeming with patients. Broken bones competed for attention with coughs, fevers, snot-nosed preschoolers, and hypochondriacs. Frank and Angie hit traffic on the way there and instead of arriving at 8:30 a.m. as planned, they checked in about 9:15 a.m.

While they were still in the emergency room, Frank broke out in a cold sweat and began to shiver. He begged for immediate attention. "I can't stop shaking," he pleaded, "You've got to get a doctor."

Someone asked if Frank had a history of seizures, he said no and was handed Tylenol. Once in the presence of a doctor, the physician took tests, looked at the results, wrote prescriptions, and offered advice.

"Get some rest, take some fluids, and take the medicine that's been prescribed."

They were there about five hours, and Angie was itching to go. She had to pick up her daughter from school.

"We left there—I think it was like 2:30 because I was like, I'm sorry I shouldn't say this, I'll get a ticket, but I was bookin' down the 60 to get my daughter."

The couple and Angie's daughter arrived back home in Montebello sometime around 3:00 p.m. where Angie inserted the Compazine suppositories that Frank required. The side effects range from drowsiness, dizziness, and lightheadedness to blurred vision, constipation, and dry mouth.

It also makes you pass out.

"At some point Frank took a turn for the worse," Angie explained once again, "he would babble just like if somebody's just totally drugged up. Like somebody is just totally out of it, you know? And I called the pharmacist, and I asked if that was normal, and he said yeah, well, if Frank isn't used to taking lots of medication, then it would be normal if you were not used to taking lots of meds plus being sick anyway."

"What pharmacist was that?"

"Huh?"

The question broke Angie's narrative flow like a rack of nails across a two-lane blacktop.

"I just wanted," explained Detective Steinwand," to know which pharmacist, what pharmacy. Kaiser? Did you call back Kaiser?"

"Kaiser."

"Is that the Kaiser in Baldwin Park? Or the Kaiser at—"

Steinwald's sudden fascination on which Kaiser Pharmacy she called certainly seemed peculiar, and Angie's response was courteous yet indicative of her view of the basic question: "I believe it was Baldwin Park, but it is easy enough to find out—I simply called the phone number of the pharmacy on the bottle."

As long as they were on the subject of medications, Angie detailed the Friday schedule. Some meds required a four-hour interval, other were to be taken every twelve hours. Between trips to the bathroom, Frank slept. He paused between those two basic needs long enough to offer prayers to the Almighty and expressions of love and gratitude to his beloved wife.

She then related the rest of the story, right up to the knock on the door of the first arriving Montebello police officer.

She described the scene and, for obvious reasons of bereavement and discomfort, she backed away from Frank's dead body on the floor and moved towards her future without Frank. She mentioned that Frank and she both had insurance policies with each other as beneficiaries.

"Is everything being taken care of there? Are you and

your daughter going to be okay?"

Angie appreciated Holmes's sincere interest in her well-being and answered honestly.

Just days before his death, Frank enjoyed a light moment helping Angie's daughter Autumn with her homework. Stepfather and daughter were described as close by all those who knew the family. (Courtesy Photo)

"Well, actually, no. The insurance won't pay out on the policy until the coroner says what the cause of death was. They are just holding up settling up on the policy until the coroner tells me or them or somebody why Frank's dead. You know, he was so healthy for sure. It's not natural to be that healthy and that dead at the same time. Well, what do I do? Sleep in my car until November? I don't have family here. But I don't want to push the coroners because of that either. I mean, even Frank's funeral is covered by a lien on the insurance policy."

"Did Frank have like some really huge—"

"Policy? No, not particularly," acknowledged Angie, "Frank took out two-fifty for his family, and even the insurance agent said it was conservative considering Frank was sole provider, plus I was going back to school. We both had policies with each other and Autumn as beneficiaries."

Angie loosed a long painful sigh. It was pretty damn obvious she just wanted this nightmare behind her, and from the way she talked, she was hoping for a geographic cure. She then began to talk about leaving LA for good.

"I want to move back to the Central Coast, to Paso Robles because half the people there are my friends," she said and then shifted the conversation back to the coroner's office. "Have you guys been successful in trying to expedite it—the coroner's investigation or testing or whatever?"

"We hope to," he said. "They, like everybody, they have a caseload, and they have a workload. We'll do the best we can."

Angie smiled for the first time in the interview.

"I believe it. I believe it. I believe you men are professionals," she said. "And, I really feel comfortable with that. I just have to have faith that between the will of the Lord and the work of professionals I can trust, it will all come together, and we'll understand."

"Yes," agreed Holmes. "'Farther along we'll understand why.'"

Angie smiled.

"I know that hymn by heart, and I've always loved it."

She proved it by humming it all the way out of the interrogation room, out of the building, and into her car.

The two detectives looked at each other, and each knew what the other was thinking. The prime suspect in the death of a married man or woman is the surviving spouse. Angie, despite her fascination with true crime television shows and the endless episodes of *Law & Order*, didn't realize that everything about her demeanor and behavior reinforced the detectives' suspicion that she murdered her husband.

This doesn't mean the detectives completely discounted Angie's allegations against Peter at Angel Gate. Real detectives are perfectly willing to be wrong if it leads them to the truth. Yes, Angie was a prime suspect, but suspicions are not convictions.

The first order of investigative business was a comprehensive questioning of Peter Robespierre, the alleged pervert at Angel Gate. The second order of business was to learn as much as possible about the personal history of Angelina Rodriguez.

Patsy Cline

The detectives carried their investigation up the California coast to the residence of Peter Robespierre.

Upon meeting the man Angie implicated in her husband's murder, they could immediately see why Angie pointed the man out as a possible suspect. He seemed like the sort of guy who might get picked up in a sting from *Dateline's To Catch a Predator*. If you called Central Casting and said, "Send me someone who looks like a pervert," this is the guy who would show up. But that was as far as the comparison went.

Although Peter appeared to be an odd duck, he was well-spoken, kindly, and more than cooperative. In truth, there had never been a complaint lodged against Peter by Frank—not to Angel Gate, nor to law enforcement.

"I'd been Frank's friend for a long time," he told detectives, "but Angie is no friend of mine, and he hasn't been for quite a while. She's a manipulator and insincere. I tried to warn Frank about her, but he wouldn't listen. He was infatuated with her, but what he saw wasn't who she was."

Encouraged to explain, Peter didn't hold back. Over the course of their discussion he told how Angelina acted before meeting Frank and how she altered her entire presentation to appeal to him.

"Angie was a chameleon. She changed her act anytime she set her eyes on a guy," said Peter. "Before she met Frank, Angie was fixated with a man at Angel Gate who had a cowboy vibe. The dude wore boots, a Stetson, jeans, and oversized sterling silver belt buckles. Well, she went after this guy with single-minded devotion. Angie took to wearing similar attire. She worked the angle hard, buying a hat and boots of her own. For a while, Angie even attempted to speak in a drawl. It looked as if Angie had him hooked, but before she could reel him in, he became interested in someone else, so she changed her bait and went fishing for Frank."

As a dedicated Christian, Frank wasn't ashamed to make his views public. Once Angie figured she wanted a piece of Frank, she dropped the country-western routine, stopped dressing like Patsy Cline, and began presenting herself more like a preacher's wife. The clothes and presentation changed, and so did the props supporting her new character. Her car suddenly sported Christian bumper stickers, a Bible was her constant companion, and she was quite adept at quoting the letters of Paul.

Angie also started attending Wednesday worship services, and while Frank was enthralled, Peter and some of Frank's other pals were more perceptive. They had seen Angie change personalities and personal presentation more than once.

"We'd seen it before," said Peter, "this was nothing new, but Frank was needy, and Angie has this lovely daughter. It was a ready-made family that Frank probably thought would give him that stable home life he always wanted."

Frank, according to Peter, believed that Angie was part of God's plan for him because Angie loved the Lord as much as he did. "Frank told me and his other friends that we were worldly and didn't understand the spiritual bond that he and Angie shared."

After talking to Peter, detectives wanted to speak to Angie's "close personal friends," assuming she had some. Detectives knew of at least one—Palmira Gorham, an outgoing woman from a large Paso Robles family that knew everyone and everyone knew them. The extended family was one of those that welcomed everyone, including Angie. She was friends with "Mira" and was treated like one of the clan.

Angie's friends described her as a chameleon who changed her attire, her attitude and hobbies to when she had her eyes set on landing a man. She went from being a wild girl to a devout Christian after meeting Frank. (Courtesy Photo)

It was Ms. Gorham who informed the two sleuths that within weeks of marrying Frank, Angie was having hot sex with Gorham's nephew, recently released from six months incarceration in the San Luis Obispo County Jail. The couple got it on about three weeks before Frank's death, and since her husband died, Angie was coming around for more as often as she could.

"I was there when Frank proposed to her," said Mira, "and I believed that they would make a fine couple. Angie did complain about the lack of sex before they were married, but after they were married, it was Angie who withheld sex from Frank—probably because she was giving it all to my nephew, Daniel."[7]

According to Mira Gorham, it didn't take long before Angie started complaining about Frank. She didn't like how strict he was with her daughter. She didn't like his insistence on attending church. She didn't like that he wanted to be in control of their finances. She specifically told Gorham that Frank wasn't loving enough and he didn't care for her or her daughter.

Mira told Steinwand and Holmes that she visited Angie in Montebello right after Frank's death and thought that Angie's reaction to his death was oddly cold.

"Then, almost as soon as Frank was buried, Angie was spending nearly all her time in Paso Robles," said Gorham, the unspoken end of that sentence being "in bed with Daniel." Perhaps her sexual focus was part of the grieving process.

Being a good friend, Mira went to Angie's to help her out following Frank's funeral. She found Angie packing up and preparing to get the hell out of town.

"Angie bitterly complained about the pace of the coroner's office and the investigation into Frank's death," recalled Mira. "She said she needed money and really wanted to take her daughter back up the coast and start life all over."

Talking to Palmira Gorham, detectives asked her if she know about this guy Peter, and did she suspect that "he or anyone else had it in for Frank?"

"The only person I ever heard say anything negative about Frank was Angie," she answered. "I told her to just divorce him just like she did all her other husbands."

"All her other husbands? How many—" the detectives were increasingly curious.

"Oh, don't you know," chided Gorham, "Marriage and

_____
7 Not his real name

divorce are common for Angie. Let's see, how many has she had? It doesn't take long to itemize them. There was the mini-marriage when she was in her teens, and then the wonderful one to Mr. Right—Tom Fuller—when she was in the Air Force. They had two daughters—one died. Horrible tragedy. That's where Angie got all her money to pay for the expensive designer label clothes, luxury cruises, and the fantastic house she owned before she married the guy she married before Frank."

Whoa. Let's rewind.

"What's this about clothes, cruises, and a fantastic house?" asked the detectives.

Okay, here we go.

It is time to reveal the astonishing story of how little Angelina from the projects became a woman of impressive wealth, or at least the trappings of wealth.

There was a time when an attractive, younger Angie lived with her husband Thomas Fuller and their two daughters near Santa Barbara. Angie had expensive tastes, set ideas, and didn't take crap from her men.

The role of suburban housewife didn't suit Angie, who was still pretty and wild. She stayed in touch with her sister and her mother. Her friends and family knew she needed drama. She got it with the birth of their second child, Alicia, on August 7, 1992.

Alicia was a preemie and had been hospitalized in the neonatal intensive care ward for several months after her birth. The baby had a host of medical problems. She suffered from apnea and bradycardia—a slower than normal heartbeat.

Even after she finally came home from the hospital, Alicia's heartbeat was monitored. Angie told her friends Alicia was a little bit behind. In fact, she didn't even start crawling until she was thirteen months.

In early 1993, Angie, Tom, and the girls visited Tom's mom and dad in Michigan. Out at a restaurant one night, Angie and the baby were the center of attention. After telling the couple how cute their little girls were, a waitress remarked on Alicia's pacifier:

"That pacifier has been recalled," she said, "because kids can choke on 'em. Seriously. There's something wrong with 'em—I think a kid choked to death on one."

"Really?"

"Really."

No, not really. No child sustained any injuries, let alone died, from sucking on the recently recalled defective Gerber pacifiers. The following March 1993 press release from Gerber contains the details, correcting the waitress's assertion that a child's death had taken place as a result of the faulty pacifier.

Gerber Products Company Recalls Gem Collection Pacifier

PRODUCT: Gerber Products Company "Gem Collection Decorator Pacifier with Travel Case," item number 76407 (single pack) or 76408 (double pack). The date codes on the back of blister packages range from 060192 (June 1, 1992) to 011893 (January 18, 1993). No other Gerber pacifiers are involved in this recall.

PROBLEM: The pacifiers may separate into pieces. The pieces could present a choking hazard to young children. No injuries have been reported.

WHAT TO DO: Consumers should immediately take the pacifiers away from young children. Call Gerber Products Company at 1-800-4-GERBER to receive a free replacement pacifier.

WASHINGTON, DC -- In cooperation with the U.S.

*Consumer Product Safety Commission (CPSC),
Gerber Products Company, Fremont, MI is
voluntarily recalling approximately 460,300 "Gem
Collection Decorator Pacifiers with Travel Case,"
manufactured between June 1992 and January 1993.
Gerber received five consumer reports that the
pacifiers separated into pieces (nipple, shield and
end cap). No injuries or chokings were reported, but
the separated pieces of the pacifiers could present a
choking hazard to young children.*

*The Gem Collection pacifiers have tan nipples, tinted
plastic shields, and plastic end caps decorated with
a marching bear with a top hat and drum, a teddy
bear with hearts, or a rabbit. The name "Gerber"
is embossed on the shields. The travel cases are
transparent, flexible plastic covers that fit directly
over the nipples.*

*The recalled pacifiers were sold in retail stores
nationwide. The single pack pacifiers sold for $2.19
to $2.99 each. The double pack pacifiers sold for
$3.99 to $4.99 each.*

Despite the heads-up on the specific pacifier's potential
danger to Alicia, Angie didn't say good-bye to the binky.
When Tom and she returned home, she brought it with her,
later stashing it at a friend's house.

Always one to better her position and acquire new skills,
Angie embarked on a new career with Prudential Insurance.
Her most significant sale was when she sold herself a
$50,000 life insurance policy on baby Alicia. The primary
beneficiary, of course, was Angie.

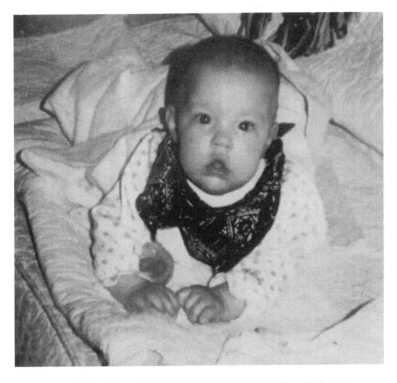

Angie's daughter Alicia Fuller died in 1993 after choking to death in her crib on a broken pacifier. Angie had a $50,000 life insurance policy on the baby. This is one of several pictures of the baby with the pacifier. (Evidence photo)

Not long after, on September 18, 1993, baby Alicia was dead.

Sometime after 11:30 a.m., a 911 call went out to Santa Barbara paramedics and first responders. A child was not breathing and unresponsive. Deputies and firefighters arrived at 11:45 a.m.

Angie was standing alone, outside the house on the well-manicured lawn, waiting for the paramedics. Firefighters arrived first, and one stayed with Angie while the crew ran into the baby's room. Engineer David Mandeville found Alicia on her back in the crib, unconscious, and not breathing.

Mandeville attempted mouth-to-mouth but noticed the toddler's airway was blocked. He stuck his finger down her throat, and after several tries was able to dislodge a rubber nipple jammed far down her throat. It fell to the floor as he continued to do everything he could to revive the baby via CPR.

When paramedics finally arrived they put the little girl in an ambulance and brought her to the hospital. Lights and sirens blazing, the men tried to save Alicia. On the way to the hospital their rescue van broke down and the paramedics waited at the side of the road before another unit could arrive.

Alicia never regained consciousness and was pronounced dead on arrival. Soon after rescue crews left, veteran Sheriff's Deputy Ralph Ginter examined Alicia's crib. He noticed the plastic backing of a pacifier laying there. He bagged it, leaving the severed rubber nipple on the floor where Mandeville had tossed it.

Ginter accompanied Angie to the hospital. Attempting to get a sense of what happened, he asked Angie some questions.

She said she put the baby to sleep at 10:30 that morning. She looked in on the baby after 11:30 and noticed she wasn't breathing. She saw that the baby had turned pale blue. She recalled that the baby felt cold and clammy to her touch.

She called 911 and waited for help.

"Then things got a little weird," recalled Ginter. "Angie, who never shed a tear after being told her baby was dead, demanded that I hand over the broken plastic backing. She was adamant about it, so I handed it over."

"They are going to pay for this," Angie shouted as if auditioning for The Little Theater. "This should never happen to another child."

"She didn't tell me," said Ginter, "that a $50,000 life insurance policy on Alicia's life took effect hours before the baby died."

The September 20 autopsy done by Dr. Wallace Carroll found that Alicia's cause of death was asphyxiation due to an obstruction of the airway. She choked to death on the plastic nipple that somehow got down her throat.

Santa Barbara County Sheriff's Deputy Claude Tuller called Angie on the twenty-second, gave her the autopsy results, and then asked if it would be possible to take some pictures of the broken pacifier. Angie referred him to her attorney. Eventually pictures were taken and the pacifier was returned.

Tom, grieving father of baby Alicia, was beyond heartbroken by the death of his infant daughter and outraged by the very idea that Gerber would allow a defective and dangerous pacifier to remain on sale at Sears to an unsuspecting public. If he found that shocking, he was undoubtedly floored by the sudden arrival of a $50,000 check.

"I was stunned," recalled Tom Fuller, "Prudential sent us a check for just over $50,000. I had no idea that Angie had taken out a policy on the baby."

Fifty-thousand dollars in not exactly a fair exchange for human life, and the influx of dollars didn't bring back Tom and Angie's little girl.

Angie and Tom filed suit against both Gerber and Sears, the store where they purchased the pacifier. A judge cut Sears loose early on, but Gerber was still on the hook.

The suit laid out the gist of the damage Alicia's death had wrought:

"Angelina Fuller suffered and will continue to suffer damages including but not limited to, shock and emotional injury and suffering in such amount as will be proven at the

time of trial."

"Gerber knew about defective pacifiers," insisted Angie, "and despite the recall notice, they did nothing to stop their sale."

The death of little Alicia was a modern American tragedy perfect for TV, especially during "sweeps week"—the most important week in the television ratings cycle—which is exactly when the local TV station aired in-depth interviews with Tom and Angie about the heartbreaking loss of their infant.

"Angie was in her element," said Tom, "I could see that she enjoyed the attention, but I thought that smiling and laughing during the interviews was inappropriate. Looking back on it now, I realize that Angie was getting off on the concern displayed by the reporter. She seemed to have a little smile on her face every once in a while, and she just seemed to enjoy the attention," he said.

The increased media attention and the stress of bereavement strained the Fuller's increasingly fragile relationship. The couple began to argue more frequently but kept a good game face for the press, and Angie was well rehearsed for all possible questions about the Gerber pacifier and the death of her beloved baby.

When asked for details, Angie had her story well-rehearsed and properly presented.

"That particular pacifier had been lost for several weeks. It had been at a friend's house, and I had just recently had it handed back to me. Of course, like any good mother, "Angie continued, "I always checked the device to make sure it wasn't sticky, overused, or dirty and that it was all in one piece, you know, I always would look at the shield to make sure it was intact, and I kind of put my fingers on it, just to make sure it wasn't loose," she said.

Angie was also well-versed in retelling the tragic story

of Alicia's death. "At around 10:30 that morning, I placed her facedown in the crib. There were no toys in there, and when Alicia got comfortable, I gave her the pacifier. Usually I would give her a bottle, but this morning was different. Alicia fell asleep right away, and I sort of tip-toed out of the room."

Several minutes later, Angie returned to check on little Alicia to make sure that she was breathing okay. "Alicia had a runny nose that week, and I had given her some baby cough syrup to dry her up and help her sleep. She was all right," said Angie, "I could hear her breathing."

When Angie checked on her, little Alicia still had the pacifier in her mouth. For a second time Angie said she tip-toed out of the room. Approximately thirty minutes later, she returned for another visit.

"I noticed the baby wasn't moving and for sure wasn't breathing. Her blankets were kicked off. She looked really different," Angie said. "Her color had turned blue and her eyes were part-way opened, but when I touched her, her skin was cold and clammy."

Angie picked up the cordless phone and dialed 911. "During the call, I noticed the broken pacifier in the crib, and I guessed that Alicia had choked on it. I tried to get it out of her throat, but I was shaking so hard and was so panicked and frantic, and I didn't pick her up right."

When Angie and her other daughter, Autumn, arrived at the hospital that afternoon, among Angie's first calls was to her sister, Gigi, in New York.

"She was horribly distraught, inconsolable, and grieving terribly over her baby that suffocated on that pacifier," remembers Angie's sister who insists that no matter what others may think, she knows that her sister would never do anything to harm Alicia.

All of the blame for baby Alicia's death was placed

on Gerber, the company that made and sold the defective pacifier. Tom and Angie launched a wrongful death law suit against Gerber. Their attorney, Barry Novak, asked Gerber for $6 million.

"The conduct of the defendants was so vile, base, contemptible, miserable, wretched, and loathsome that it would be looked down upon and despised by ordinary decent people."

Gerber's lawyers took an assumed risks tack, insisting that the baby's death was the Fuller's fault because Angie and Tom failed to exercise due care of the child. Gerber asked the Santa Maria judge to dismiss the case.

In response, Angie's attorney said he would call the coroner, the paramedics, and emergency personnel to be deposed. They would explain how the little girl died and how it left her parents distraught. He promised to call calloused Gerber employees too, ensuring a jury of Central California working stiffs would see an aggrieved parent wronged by the system.

"The multi-million-dollar lawsuit," says expert Fred Wolfson, "pitted an unwitting all-American family against a mighty but unfeeling multinational company making its inhuman decisions overseas at their headquarters in Germany, making Gerber sound as if it were the evil corporate love child of Goebbels and Goering."

It began with a simple declaration: "The product involved in this case is a Gerber Gem Collection Decorator Pacifier with Travel Case and its component parts."

It's easy to see how any family would assume that a Gerber pacifier was safe for their children, and the Fuller's civil action made it clear that the loss of a baby daughter to something so seemingly innocent would be costly.

"By reason of decedent's death, descendant's power to earn and accumulate money and property has been destroyed."

Angie's turn to spin the death came next. The agony—real or imagined—was palpable.

"The plaintiff witnessed the incident, injuries, and damages to her daughter Alicia Fuller while within the zone of danger."

The turn of phrase—zone of danger—is an interesting choice. It's a strictly legal term that can be applied to cases involving negligent infliction of emotional distress. The phrase itself comes from a 1928 ruling that defined modern tort cases in terms of liability and damages. Essentially the doctrine allows for recovery of damages to people in a "dangerous area." Typically, the "dangerous area" is caused by a defendant's negligence, and it extends to those who suffered harm as a result of the defendant's negligence.

Basically if you did something that hurt somebody you are going to have to pay for that hurt. The lawsuit went on to explain just how Angie was hurt by the death of her daughter.

"Plaintiff Angelina Fuller received some physical and mental injuries from this incident as a result of witnessing said injuries and damages."

Clearly no parent wants to find his or her infant child dead in a crib. And a parent encountering that sort of situation is clearly entitled to be compensated. The only question that remained was how much compensation would be enough. It wasn't just finding the baby dead that hurt Angie, there would be lingering emotional damage

"(Angie) suffered and will continue to suffer damages including but not limited to, shock and emotional injury and suffering in such amount as will be proven at the time of trial," the suit pointed out. Angie said she was entitled to "future medical, psychological, and related expenses all to plaintiff's damage in such amount as will be proven at the time of trial."

It all came down to trust. If a parent such as Angie was unable to trust the maker of a product as benign as a "binky," a company whose slogan is "Babies are our business," who is there left to trust?

Angie trusted Gerber, and what made matters worse was that Gerber knew there was a problem for a long time prior to the recall and Alicia's death. The lawsuit's intended *coup de gras* pointed to reports that a year before Alicia's death, Gerber knew there was a problem with the pacifier and its potential to separate. Gerber knew that if a nipple would separate from the shield it would present a choking hazard to an infant.

The proof was in the stats. Angie's complaint included those too.

"Gerber Products Company manufactured 690,192 of these pacifiers, of which 229,914 were in Gerber's warehouse as of February 1993 and 460,278 had been distributed. On or about February 5, 1993, Gerber sent a voluntary recall notice to their customers requesting that the products be removed. Only 25 percent were recovered from distributors leaving 75 percent of the dangerous and defective pacifiers either in the stream of distribution or in the hands of customers unaware of the choking hazard posed by this particular product's design and manufacture."

What Gerber did, or neglected to do, may not be an actual crime, but the suit presented it as bordering on criminality.

Gerber wasn't eager to battle grieving parents in the harsh light of a public courtroom, and rather than be cast as baby killers, Gerber decided to settle quietly and get that damn irritating Angelina Fuller out of their corporate hair.

Drugs, Dollars, and Domestic Violence

Angelina was fond of low-cut dresses that showed off her figure. She posed for this photo just about the time she and Tom Fuller were married. (Courtesy Photo)

Angie and Tom still had their marriage to settle. The couple had moved from Lompoc and were living in Santa

Maria in a two-story stucco house. A bough covered with flowers framed the front entrance. Cypress trees stood on the property line. The couple and their growing daughter lived in a typical suburban house in a typical suburban neighborhood.

Tom and Angie were out of the military. He was selling nutrition supplements. Her friends said when Tom was out of town Angie chased meaningless sexual liaisons, tried to dull her mind with prescription drugs, and in between it all attempted to sell insurance out of a Prudential office in a mini-mall on the main road between Santa Maria and Lompoc.

Married on June 15, 1990, the couple was sick of each other by June 1994. Angie, hooked on prescription painkillers and snorting occasional lines of homemade peanut butter crank, filed for divorce in October, got herself a boyfriend, and moved into the Rose Place apartments. The shabby collection of three courtyard-style apartment complexes backs up to the 101 in a tougher part of Santa Maria.

The property Tom and Angie split was miniscule. She got some appliances, a 1991 Geo Metro, and whatever proceeds might come out of another lawsuit she filed up in San Luis Obispo. She asked for half of the Gerber settlement.

Tom got to keep the couple's house in Santa Maria, a 1988 Camaro, $6,000 in credit card debt, and half the Gerber settlement—when it became final. That would change.

Ultimately the ploy for attention proved somewhat lucrative. Gerber settled out of court with Tom and Angie. A portion of the settlement agreement was sealed per Gerber's request.

The now-divorced couple divided $710,000. Angie said she was far more hurt than Tom and insisted she get more money. Ultimately she took 60 percent, and Tom got the leftovers. After attorney's fees and court costs that meant a $246,000 windfall for Angie. Tom's share was $164,000.

Angie said she deserved more because she found the baby dead and it caused her a greater amount of emotional trauma.

Even her divorce case focused less on the irreconcilable differences she claimed she and Tom experienced and more on her lack of funds.

Within the divorce documents Angie reported a monthly income of $625 and expenses of $1,394. She claimed she didn't know what Tom made selling muscle-building supplements.

Despite the disparity between her income and her expenses, Angie said she had $100 in a checking account. As for her expenses? The list included $425 for monthly rent, $150 for food, $25 for eating out, $70 for utilities, $90 for her telephone, $20 for laundry and cleaning, and $60 for insurance. She said she spent nothing on entertainment and $50 a month on gas. Angie also listed installment payments to Gottschalks, Sears, and Fingerhut totaling about $100 a month.

You have to wonder if the installment payments to Sears included the cost of the pacifier. As for Fingerhut, it makes sense Angie was buying stuff out of the low-budget, easy credit catalog. Fingerhut in the early 1990s was a powerhouse of marketing to a certain strata of the consumer marketplace. Angie—in debt up to her eyeballs and straining to acquire material possessions—fit the profile.

Looking back, Tom said he could see the storm clouds on the horizon of their rocky marriage. "Angie became obsessed with our daughters' afterlives," he said. "She insisted on baptism."

"There is no way Angie had anything to do with her baby's death. I would stake my life on it," insists her sister, Gigi. "She really is a good person. She wouldn't do anything to hurt anybody. She could never do something like that. She's not smart enough. I can't imagine what would possess her."

Angie's possessions were material. And with the money from Gerber and Angie's other income-producing talents, Angie was able to live it up, although her taste in lovers took a step down from the handsome athletic and ethical Thomas Fuller.

Following the divorce, Angie took up with a small-time crook with a big reputation for minor incidents and adequate amounts of amphetamines to keep them jockeying for position in the world of sexual pyrotechnics.

Their sexual compatibility kept them together but things soon turned sticky. In March 1995 she called Santa Maria Police after he allegedly broke into their apartment.

"(He) illegally entered my home while I was not home," Angie wrote in a declaration seeking a restraining order. Her cramped writing was without style. Simple, block print gave her side of things.

"When I arrived home with a friend he was in my bedroom. I insisted he leave but he refused. He then took a necklace of mine, spit in my face, told me to watch my back and left. I immediately called the SMPD. Officer Mike Schroder came to my home took a report then arrested (him) at his home for illegal entry and battery on my person."

Feeling sorry for her former lover, Angie told the cops she didn't want to file charges. "I dropped the charges due to he told me he would seek help because he was using crank and did not realize what he was doing."

The report came at a time of heightened awareness about spousal abuse. The murder trial of former football great O.J. Simpson was in full swing. Simpson, a Pro Football Hall of Fame running back, was accused of slashing his ex-wife and her friend to death outside a Brentwood condominium the summer before.

By March 1995, the Simpson case was ubiquitous. The

overarching theme that emerged was that Simpson was a wife abuser. Laws were changed, police responses were modernized, and women were urged to turn on their abusers.

So who could blame Angie for trying to be a part of the Simpson drama even if she was a couple hundred miles away? Fact is, Simpson was on every television set and part of every watercooler conversation in 1995.

A month after she refrained from filing a case against her estranged boyfriend, Angie was on the phone with the police again. She explained what happened in an application for a restraining order filed in the Santa Maria courthouse that was about a mile south of her apartment.

"After speaking with him about staying away from me, he physically grabbed my face and bruised it. Then he cracked the dashboard of my car," Angie wrote.

Her printing style made each word stand out. She explained how her surviving daughter was at risk and made sure to bring up life insurance.

"He told me to make sure I have insurance coverage so my daughter would be provided for in my absence," Angie continued. "I filed a report again with the Santa Maria Police Department. Nothing has been done with that. Since such time I have received numerous threatening phone calls from him. He has called Tom Fuller, ex-husband, and left numerous degrading and threatening statements. I have the recent fifteen-plus messages recorded for further reference."

Any day at the Santa Maria courthouse, a constant stream of women come to the clerk's desk seeking the paperwork they need to get a restraining order. Some are sent to the courthouse by the police, others are brought by friends.

One afternoon a woman said she came down because she wanted her boyfriend out of her damn house. He's a prison guard in Bakersfield, she explained. He carries a gun. She wanted him served at work so he wouldn't go nuts on her and the children.

The lone man who came to the counter that morning seeking a restraining order against a friend with whom he lived, said he was sent by the police. He decided to back out when the clerk explained how much the legal documentation would cost.

Angie didn't have that problem. Tucked in her legal file was a court order declaring her too poor to afford court costs. Her restraining order was granted and set in place for three years.

The tiff with the boyfriend was one of many legal battles Angie was fighting in Santa Maria following the death of Alicia.

Angie invoked sympathy by sharing the depths of her degradation and despair growing up as a "victim." While there is no doubt that Angie was exploited by her grandfather, a cousin, and others who preyed on her during her teen years, she couldn't resist enhancing the facts with a heavy layer of additional drama, accompanied by outright fabrication rendering the truth of any particular reported recollection highly suspect.

Some of Angie's lying was the result of a survival-oriented perspective on life. As is common with others who shared similar childhoods, Angie consistently acted to protect herself without consideration of the negative consequences of her actions on other people.

Even when offered less destructive behavioral options, Angie seemed to always do exactly what she felt was in her best interest, sexually and financially.

"Her post-divorce intercourse," commented satiric journalist Travis Webb, "climaxed in an uncordial disconnect. Hard feelings were all that remained after Angie terminated her over-stimulated lovers' all access pass to her well-worn pathways of pleasure."

Flush with booty from Gerber, Angie spread her wealth by getting a leg up on California's Central Coast wine country. Her new home was lavish, clothes expensive, car luxurious, and the purchase of a boat was, by her own admission, an unnecessary extravagance.

"Angie knows how to spend money," confirmed Suzie Pinkham. "She can also sniff it out like a pig rooting for truffles."

Another woman impressed by Angie's lifestyle was Betty Hailey. The two met in 1997 at a school-bus stop. Angelina recently listed her well-landscaped, four-bedroom home in Paso Robles. It was Hailey who purchased the home that Angie bought with the Gerber settlement money, and soon the two women were fast friends. "Whatever she wanted, she bought," Hailey says. "We prayed together, babysat for one another, and when she married Frank, I was her matron of honor."

"My husband and I went on a cruise with Angie," confides a former friend, "I didn't dare leave my husband alone with her for five minutes for fear she'd be having sex with him by minute number six."

"Despite our friendship," Hailey remarked, "I never really trusted her completely. She was very impulsive. When she found out my son was single, she invited herself to his Washington, DC, home for Thanksgiving."

Hailey, who no longer lives in Angie's old home in Paso Robles, admits that in the final analysis, Angelina was more than a mystery,

"I prayed with her and I counseled with her, but to tell you the truth, I didn't know that much about her."

Neither did Frank Rodriguez. There is little doubt that Frank was unaware of exactly how many husbands preceded him in holy matrimony to Angelina. There was another marriage between Tom Fuller and Frank Rodriguez.

Angie was also married briefly to a Mr. Combs who, to his credit, didn't buy life insurance. Angie divorced him in a matter of months.

"You divorced everyone else you've married," said Palmira when Angie started complaining about Frank. "What's the difference this time?"

"Nope. Can't do it, Angie said. "This one has a life insurance policy. If I were to kill him at least I'd get a little money."

Palmira's mother, Helen Morones, overheard the conversation and offered her own take on the situation. She remembered watching a TV show or reading a story about a woman who wanted to kill her husband and used oleander to do it.

It may not have happened in real life as oleander is a common device used by mystery novelists to kill off unsuspecting victims. Then, almost by magic, the novelist's master detective figures out the case via a combination of brilliant deduction, suave interrogation and—after surviving an attempt on his or her own life—sheer luck.

Maybe that's what Helen heard. Whatever it was, she ran it all down for Angie and Mira as they sat at her kitchen table.

"She tried to kill him with a tea made from oleander."

Angie said she had never heard of it. Helen explained that it was the flower on a bush you see all over California.

"It is a deadly poison," Helen said before adding an admonishment. "It didn't work for that woman, though. She ended up getting caught and going to jail."

Mira continued to speak to detectives about her friend.

"Angie and I laughed at the woman's misfortune," Mira told the two detectives. "The topic of conversation shifted. Angie went off with Daniel to, as usual, have sex."

Steinwand and Holmes interviewed him next, but the

much maligned man didn't have much to say.

"I told Angie that I didn't mind screwing her once in a while, but I wanted no part of killing anyone. No way in hell. The more I thought about it the more I thought Angie was one of two things: someone making rude jokes or a serious stone cold killer. I mean, I thought it was like a running gag, because murdering Frank was a frequent topic of conversation."

Angie seemed to like the idea of poisoning Frank. Everyone had their ideas about which poison worked best. At some point the conversation focused on a neighbor's dogs. One had got loose and went after Mira's young son. She called the police.

"Of course, the cops didn't do anything about it," she told Angie.

Mira's boyfriend, as helpful as he was handsome, chimed in with some advice of his own.

"We could just soak some hot dogs in antifreeze and throw it over the fence," he said.

"Antifreeze?" It was Angie asking. She was suddenly intrigued.

"We seen something on TV," chimed in an ungrammatical Mira, "that antifreeze has like kind of a sweet taste and it's really colorful, so it's like bright pink or green … and that children and animals, they would drink it without thinking twice."

Mira and her boyfriend decided against killing the neighbor's dog, but Mira remembered the conversation perfectly.

"Angie must have filed away information about oleander and antifreeze in her mind. She was no dummy. I called her up one day," said Mira. "There was a sound in the background that made it difficult to hear. It sounded like a jackhammer, and I asked her what it was. "

"It's the blender," Angie answered. "I'm making Frank a *special* milkshake. You know he likes them when he's not feeling well."

"Is he sick?" Gorham asked as the blender whirring stopped.

"Not yet," Angie answered

Mira picked up on the malevolent lilt in Angie's intonation, the one she used every time she talked about killing Frank.

"It was a running joke that had run out of humor by then," said Mira. "It wasn't funny anymore, and it was starting to sound as if she weren't joking, and that made it even more uncomfortable."

As if that were not enough hearsay and gossip about Angie and Frank to titillate the detective duo, Daniel then shared with the investigators a chilling conversation he had with Angie.

"I never said anything about this before," he confided, "but Angie told me that she had loosened gas lines around the dryer and water heater back in Montebello in hopes that Frank would either suffocate from the toxic fumes or that the house would blow up."

It didn't work.

In fact, her plan was completely botched. Frank smelled the leak and called Southern California Gas Company.

Technician Luis Aguilar got the call. He was dispatched to Frank's residence, and almost as soon as he arrived he got a whiff of rotten eggs.

"The smell comes from an additive added to natural gas and propane," explains Aguilar. "Without it, the toxic and highly explosive gasses would be odorless as well as colorless. So as a warning of potential problems, it's added to the gasses as a precaution. Bad smell equals bad problems.

Frank and Angelina were married in a religious ceremony attended by family and friends. Just weeks after moving to suburban Los Angeles, a gas leak at the couple's home nearly resulted in Frank's death. (Courtesy Photo)

Frank was happy to see Aguilar and pointed him to the clothes dryer at the back of the garage. As he got closer to the dryer, the snake-like gas hose hissed the obnoxious rotten-egg odor at him.

"This is a pretty loose connection," Aguilar told Frank. He tightened the nut at the end of the hose, making a three-quarter turn before the hissing stopped and the leak was no more.

The smell, however, remained. Next to the dryer, the water heater, also a gas appliance, was noticeably leaking natural gas.

"It was obvious that something wasn't right," Aguilar would later recall. "The hose was really loose. Frank didn't seem concerned that it couldn't have happened on its own. I even mentioned that you couldn't have both of those things disconnected like that by accident, but it didn't seem to register."

The attempt on Frank's life frightened Daniel.

"When Angie told me about that gas leak thing," Daniel told detectives, " I didn't want to know any more. I did ask her why she was so damn bitter. She said that when they got together, everything was okay, but somewhere along the line she decided that Frank was too possessive with her and too strict with her daughter. Eventually she felt as if she had enough. She said 'He is everything; I am nothing. I just want out.'"

The interviews with Mira and Daniel complete, Steinwand and Holmes wanted to talk to Peter once more.

"We had a pretty good idea of what we needed from Peter," said Steinwand. "We flat out told him that we needed his help setting a trap for Angelina. He agreed. The play was about to begin."

Steinwand called Angie to arrange a meeting. He and Holmes wanted to plan out with her how they would build their case against Peter. The idea was to make Angie an integral part of the strategy leading to the arrest and conviction of Peter Robespierre.

"If Angie believed that we believed her suspicions about Peter—that it was Peter who was responsible for Frank's death—she would do everything she could to help us find out how Peter killed him. What he used and how it worked. In other words, we were going to use her to catch herself and help put herself on death row."

U.S. history is laced with characters like Lavinia Fisher, an eighteenth century serial killer. She and her husband, John, owned an inn outside Charleston, South Carolina. They would lure men into the home and then ply them with a concoction brewed from oleander leaves. When the poisoned men would pass out they would be robbed and killed. The plot was uncovered when a man escaped their clutches and alerted police.

Lavinia became the first woman in U.S. history to receive the death penalty. She and her husband were hanged for their deadly use of oleander.

Oleander, despite being deadly, is commonly used in landscaping in California. Hillsides, backyards, freeway dividers, and farm fences are covered in the flowering bush. It's one of those cheap landscaping makeover tools that's cost effective, large, and functional. Most importantly, oleander is drought resistant. There's not one county in California that doesn't put the plant to use for one reason or another.

Because a single bush can grow to an enormous size, crews with the California Department of Transportation, a.k.a. Caltrans, usually cut back the plant every couple of years. Along the freeway in the San Gabriel Valley back in the 1980s and early 1990s that cutback meant boom times for the hookers working North Garvey—a frontage road along the 10 Freeway.

The girls would line up along the fence, flash a little tit, or give drivers a wink and a wave. If the girls didn't cause any accidents that required assistance from the California Highway Patrol, they'd be flush with customers for most of the morning commute.

The city fathers and Caltrans eventually got wise. First they tore down the seedy motels the girls and their trolling clients used for fifteen-minute rush hour assignations. Wal-Mart was the respectable replacement business of choice. That didn't quite work out as planned, as there were unexpected "Red Light" Specials in the parking lot.

Finally, someone decided to cut down the oleander for good and put up a wall. Now there's nothing to see but Wal-Mart's sign.

The deadly fact is that poison works, and a higher percentage of murderers get away with poisoning their intended victims than murderers who use other means. Consider this interesting statistic: Of the 11,242 homicides that occurred in Los Angeles County between 2000 and 2010, just six involved victims who were poisoned. Five of those came from one family. They were gassed to death by a man intent on killing his loved ones.

The case was a sad one. Recently separated Adair Javier Garcia was so mad at his ex-wife he set out to kill himself and their six children as they slept in the tiny wood-frame and stucco Pico Rivera home the family shared.

He closed the windows of the single-story house, fired up a barbecue, and let the air inside fill with poisonous carbon monoxide gas.

Before it all went down Garcia videotaped a message to his wife. With a camera rolling, Garcia explained his plan in detail.

"I love you. I'm of sound mind, and I know what I'm doing," Garcia said. "I just want to let you know this is the only option available. You've broken me. You don't care, so I don't care. ... What I'm about to commit is the most cowardly, selfish act possible."

A separate video had recordings of each child telling their mother good-bye. Defending her client against a death penalty rap, attorney Jill Thomas called a psychiatrist who explained that Garcia killed because he was depressed and delusional. The doctor said Garcia believed that he and the children would—in death—fly away together with Peter Pan to Never Never Land.

Killed were Brenda, ten; Jonathan, seven; Anthony, two; Cecilia, four; and Vanessa, six. A nine-year-old child survived with Garcia.

But for a fluke, the deadly plan might have worked out

for Garcia. The children's grandmother rolled up on the house with plans to babysit that morning. When she saw smoke coming from it, she dialed 911. Cops and paramedics rolled, rescuing the still-alive Garcia, the surviving daughter, and six-year-old Vanessa, who was still barely breathing.

Because it was so cold that month, investigators initially believed Garcia was the idiot many fear—the guy who heats his house with a barbecue, accidentally killing everyone. Eventually his stories didn't add up to anything other than murder.

Trial in the case lasted several days. Prosecutors hoped to get the death penalty. After all, they argued, Garcia had committed multiple murders—he killed his five children and used poison to do it. A jury didn't agree. Instead Garcia was sentenced to life in prison without the possibility of parole.

David Wayne Sconce, a Pasadena mortician, was accused of killing a rival funeral parlor director with oleander. He arranged an unusual plea deal that resulted in a lifetime parole. But Sconce ultimately went to prison, not for killing—or for the horrible management of his funeral parlor—but attempting to sell a rifle to a pawn shop in Montana.

At the time Frank died, Angie was a regular viewer of numerous true crime TV shows and was very familiar with the tale of Alexei and Peter Wiltsey. Toddlers, the pair died in the spring of 2000 after eating oleander they picked in a neighbor's backyard. Scott Carrier, a spokesman for the Los Angeles County Department of Coroner said the deaths were the county's first ever attributed to accidental oleander ingestion.

Dan Anderson and Michelle Sandberg with the coroner's department studied the case and put together a slideshow for other criminalists and lab techs to explain what happened.

Essentially the boys, Russian adoptees, were malnourished. Three-year-old Alexei at twenty-eight pounds was in the fifth percentile in weight. Two-year-old Peter at twenty-six pounds in the second.

Over four days the boys probably ate leaves from the neighbor's oleander twice. The first time, a Monday, their mother observed them spitting out green leafy material and exclaiming "yucky," Anderson and Sandberg wrote.

That night both children were nauseated and vomiting.

On Tuesday the two were "under the weather." Although Alexei regained his appetite, Peter was lethargic.

By Wednesday the kids were playing around again, and although their grandmother saw Peter carrying an oleander sprig, she thought nothing of it.

Wednesday night Peter and Alexei ate dinner with the family. On Thursday morning they were dead. A check of the house turned up a towel with vomit that contained a green leafy substance.

Anderson and Sandberg would conclude the children suffered from a condition known as "pica."

Pica "afflicts malnourished children and causes them to compulsively eat dirt, paint chips, or other non-food substances," the two wrote.

The recollection of neighbors helped piece it all together. Folks who knew the toddlers told investigators: "The boys were hungry." "Could not believe how much they ate." "They would polish everything off." "If something fell on the floor, they would find it and eat it," Anderson and Steinberg reported.

The story was all over the newspapers. Reporters tracked the case from May through September. The *Los Angeles Times* played it big, with a bylined story on the front of the Metro section, when the autopsy was finalized in July.

The story by Jessica Garrison included these paragraphs:

"(The parents) said that when they found leaf particles in the boys' vomit three days before their deaths, they didn't immediately suspect that they had eaten poisonous plants. "'I wasn't thinking plants,' (the mother) said. ... 'If I had known it was oleander, we would have had them to the doctor so fast it would have made your head spin.'"

One can conclude from a Google search, a run-through of newspaper archives, and other sources that oleander, while effective, is either seldom used by killers or seldom detected by pathologists

On the other hand, antifreeze, specifically ethylene glycol, can also be an effective poison. And, it gets a lot more press. After all, wives have been killing their husbands with it for several decades now. It tastes sweet like a sports drink and often is even the same glowing green color as stuff that might get dumped on a coach's head after a big win on the football field.

For the purposes of newspapers, antifreeze is an easier concoction to explain to readers than pretty flowers, which happen to be poisonous. Tabloid headlines in 1982 for example told the story of Shirley Allen who "iced her husband with antifreeze."

The iced husband in question, Lloyd Allen, was actually Shirley's sixth. Her fourth husband also died under mysterious circumstances, and the third left her after he discovered she was attempting to poison him.

Following Lloyd's death, Shirley, a.k.a. "The Missouri Black Widow," attempted to cash a $25,000 life insurance policy. It made the authorities suspicious—especially considering her history with men. Shirley had been married six times—five of her husbands died on her.

Shirley had previous bad luck with life insurance policies. After the death of her fourth husband in February 1978, she tried to collect on a $17,000 life insurance policy. Shirley was denied the dough after she got caught forging the man's will.

Shirley and Lloyd were married on September 25, 1981. Lloyd was dead on Nov. 1, 1981. When she was questioned by police, Shirley's daughter from a previous marriage spilled the beans. She told detectives that Mommy poisoned Stepdad's beer with antifreeze.

Shirley's daughter, Norma Hawkins, also said she saw her mom give Lloyd Allen antifreeze in soft drinks and in small containers of cough syrup.

"She stated that defendant had been doing this at least two months prior to Lloyd Allen's death," Missouri court records show.

Even Allen's neighbors suspected she was poisoning her husband.

"People were talking about it, saying she was poisoning him, but it was all joking around," one neighbor told reporters. "But we're not joking now."

Taking the stand in her own defense, Allen denied she had anything to do with her husband's untimely demise.

"I don't know who did it," she said.

Like Frank Rodriguez, Allen's last day was characterized by a fit of vomiting.

He awoke feeling sick at 3:30 a.m. Shirley refused to take him to the hospital.

There was lots of antifreeze in the Allen house. On the stand Shirley explained Lloyd kept it around to kill "rats that were coming out of the patio." The only rat they found was Shirley.

Ultimately she admitted that although Lloyd died around 4:00 a.m., she waited until nearly 11:00 a.m. before bothering to call the police.

In 1994, the case of Bobbie Jan Nicholson, a forty-nine-year-old woman from Arkansas, made headlines when it was alleged she poisoned her husband with antifreeze in hopes of inheriting his $600,000 estate.

Authorities initially thought Bobbie Jan's husband died of a heart attack. His children insisted on an autopsy and an alert medical examiner honed in on ethylene glycol—the ingredient that makes antifreeze effective.

Maybe the classic antifreeze story comes not out of a murder, but an attempted murder.

Sandra Kaye Baker, thirty, of Texarcana, Arkansas, pleaded guilty to attempted murder after she was caught trying to kill her husband with antifreeze.

Her purpose? Collecting on a $2.5 million life insurance policy.

An Associated Press story published nationally reported detectives found notes indicating she wanted to use the money to buy a four-bedroom house, land, and a swimming pool.

The kicker, according to prosecutor Brent Haltom?

"She set aside $8,000 for his funeral," Haltom said. "That was nice."

Experts who study poisoning murders say in most instances the motive comes down to one of two things, love or money.

The cable crime shows of the early 2000s feasted on these tales of husband killers. Angie would have seen them. The shows were ubiquitous. What Angie didn't suspect was that, with the help of Steinwand and Holmes, she was about to enter the pantheon of notorious husband killers.

"We befriended her. We basically led her on, so to speak, throughout the entire investigation. By the time we reached this point in the investigation, we decided we needed to tape record absolutely everything."

"We can't solve this case without you, Angie,"

"You know I'll do anything to help," Angie assured them, as if she were a guest star from *Law & Order* showing up on *CSI*.

"We want you to help us plan how we are going to nail this guy," said Steinwand, "We plan on getting a search warrant for his place. The problem is, we still don't know what kind of poison we should be looking for."

It was a softball, teed up and ready for Angie to smash out of the park. She played dumb.

"It could be the flowers at the side of the road," she answered.

After giving her some breathing room, and to avoid pressuring her to the point where she would become suspicious, they once again called on her for her insights and ideas.

"We're really interested in your suspect," Steinwand said. "But we need to know more. The coroner's office especially needs to know what you think might have been used to poison Frank. What was that poisonous plant you brought up?"

Angie said she couldn't remember the name.

"It's that plant that grows in the middle of the freeway with red and white flowers," she replied in a somewhat exasperated tone of voice.

Steinwand's partner, Holmes, had a way with suspects such as Angie. He knew how to play them and get the most out of an interview.

Angie had prepped the detectives to go after Peter Robespierre by painting him as a recalcitrant pervert with a marked propensity for pubescent flesh and a hair trigger temper ready to explode at any threat of exposure. Hence, she alleged, Peter hated Frank for raising concerns about inappropriate and non-accidental groping of Angel Gate's underage clientele. Holmes wanted to know more from Angie. He asked about the guy she wanted them to focus on as Suspect Number One. Holmes played Angie like he might a wild trout on the end of a fly line.

"You know what we're thinking about him, Angie. And you know what he is. He is really a strange bird."

"I know he is," Angie cooed.

"He is, huh?" Holmes interjected. "We were talking to him, you know, and we started reading this guy and what we need to do is," he paused for a second to gauge Angie's reaction, then continued, "You were saying that there might be some ... see, we got no way to get into his house right now."

The reactions were a series of monosyllabic responses.

"Right," Angie said, not knowing she was about to be hooked.

"We got no way," Holmes continued.

"Right," she said again.

"To get in legally."

"Right."

Holmes explained why that would be important. Naturally it involved the coroner's inability to determine how Frank died. He set the hook.

"Unless we know what we're searching for and our problem is right now we just got off the phone with the coroner's office. We're trying to find out what possible poison. Now if we could narrow it down to what possible poison, I could possibly get into his house."

"Uh-huh," Angie replied. "No word yet?"

Holmes continued with his explanation. He was going to talk to Angie's suspect again, but he wanted to go over some stuff with her first.

"I'll tell you what, we'll be there at nine o'clock tomorrow, and I'll tell you about what he said and then our suspicions and—and everything."

Angie stayed focused on the coroner's report. She wanted to know if there was any word.

"Well, they don't have anything yet. It takes time for this

type of stuff."

"Oh," Angie said.

"You know unless they know what they are looking for," Joe Bob said, his voice trailing off.

"Right," Angie said.

"Unless they know what they are looking for," he continued. "But I'll tell you what, let me get back to you."

"OK ... and if you want to come earlier just call me beforehand," Angie offered.

"Give it some thought. What you think he might've, you know something—what possibly he could have been poisoned with, you never know," Holmes said, implying that Frank's weird friend might be capable of anything.

The words began to flow. Angie reverted to complete sentences.

"It could be anything. It could be the flowers on the road. It could be something that's been ..."

"The flowers on the road?" Holmes again asked for clarification.

"Those, uh, what the heck are those? You know the— they grow—they grow in the middle of the highway. They are all over the place."

"I don't know," Holmes interrupted.

Angie claimed she'd been at the library researching all the ways someone like Frank could just keel over and die. The answer, according to all her research, had to be those pink, red, and white flowers along the road.

"I've only found this out because I started doing research myself at the library. Maybe you should go look at the library yourself. I'm just trying to be helpful and just throwing things out there. It could be flowers on the roadside. It could be something Peter bought at the store."

Realizing she may have been too specific, Angie began to back away from the flowers on the road as a potential poison.

"Well, give it some thought—give it some thought and if you remember the name of whatever that—a flower or whatever …"

Angie didn't like the turnaround. She went back to single word responses.

"Uh huh."

"Yeah."

Holmes said he wanted to follow up and ended the call. Angie was the last one to say good-bye.

On Oct. 9, 2000, Steinwand and Holmes rolled out to Angie's house in Montebello with the intent of interviewing the widow once again.

Steinwand walked up and rang the bell. When no one answered the door, Steinwand and Holmes began poking around, peeking through the windows.

The weather-worn California ranch house had been emptied in a hurry. Trash was piled up out front. They pawed through it. Angie tossed Frank's stuff like it was picked-over crap that couldn't be sold at the flea market or picked up by the Goodwill. His clothes, pictures, little things we all save to remind us of a fun day, an interesting event, people close to us—those were tossed too.

"No doubt about it, Angie didn't miss Frank," commented Fred Wolfson, "Tossing his stuff like that? Callous, contemptible, and all-around pretty fucked up. Whatever dignity Frank had in life meant nothing to Angie."

The detectives were beginning to believe Angie just looked at her dead husband as nothing more than a means to a paycheck, a $250,000 deposit in her bank account, a new house up in Paso Robles and a worry-free life, where she could hook up with Daniel or whomever and forget all about the relative dump where she lived in LA.

*Detectives believed this highly poisonous oleander plant
may have contributed to Frank's death. The plant was
growing in a neighbor's yard. (Evidence Photo)*

When they were done marveling at Angie's callousness,
Steinwand and Holmes decided to check out the backyard.
Steinwand popped open the gate and took a look around.

"I saw a large oleander tree growing up over the south
fence at the location," he later said. "There was a wood fence
bordering the south side of the yard. The yard to the south of
it was lower. It was, I guess, a little drop off to the neighbor's
backyard. The tree was growing up next to the fence along
with another—I believe it was a bougainvillea-type tree—
was growing up over the fence, which I would estimate four,
four-and-a-half-feet tall, quite a large (oleander) tree."

The leaves and flowers of the oleander reached over the fence and hung in Angie and Frank's backyard within reach of anyone who wanted to pick them and perhaps use the greenery in a tea.

Could an adult reach those leaves?

"Yes. Easily," Steinwand said.

One of the detectives took a sample and sent it off for analysis. They bagged Frank's stuff too. If Angie didn't care, the detectives did.

They called the coroner and asked investigators to figure out how to test their tissue samples for signs of oleander poisoning.

Supervising criminalist Anderson said he was relieved to have something to investigate.

"We needed a little bit of help," he said. "You kind of have to know what you are looking for first before you can identify it on the instrument."

Anderson knew for sure that Frank hadn't been poisoned with pesticide. The samples they took from his house didn't match the tissue samples they had in the lab.

"The results came back negative," he said.

Steinwand didn't let that hinder the investigation one bit, and he had an interesting conversation with Midland Insurance analyst Kim Matheson. Matheson had been working for the firm since 1979. It would be up to her to decide whether or not Angie was getting paid for Frank's death. Matheson kept pretty good notes.

"Frank's policy took effect on July 18th. So, yes," Matheson confirmed, "the insurance was in full effect on the day Frank died. Angelina, as the primary beneficiary, stands to receive a check for $250,000, but unless there is a death certificate there won't be a payout."

No payout. Period. Plain and simple. This did not bode well for Angie and her daughter. No husband, no job, and no life insurance dough for Angie meant she was about to be facing lean and tough times. The reality of it all must have begun to sink in at that point.

If she waited it out, eventually she might get paid. But, she might not get paid either. That would mean she killed Frank for nothing.

Despite the anxiety and the juggling and the sleepless nights and the dealing with the family and the police and the coroner and just about anyone else who had questions, Angie was determined that she was smarter than the police.

She told more than one acquaintance that she believed the police were a bunch of small-town hicks. They needed guidance. They needed help. She would provide the guidance and the help and point them in the right direction. That direction being the false arrest and conviction of Peter for the murder of her husband,

If it worked out, she would stay out of prison and collect $250,000 plus interest. It would be enough for a cozy home on the Central Coast. She could forget about Frank, settle down again, and feel safe.

"Money was always a big deal to Angie," said Suzie Pinkham. "As a teenager she took money from her grandpa when he forced her to have sex. Twice she got pregnant and he paid for her abortions, then gave her a little extra cash on the side for her trouble.

Money made Angie's world go 'round, and she wasn't going to let some inconvenience such as an insurance company's rules, regulations, and policies keep her away from money that was rightfully hers.

Angie became increasingly pro-active, getting on the line with the coroner, and she continued pointing the finger of blame at Peter, the man who had a grudge against her now-dead husband.

"I'm going to teach these hillbilly cops a thing or two

about murder investigation," she told Suzie, "I'm fed up with the lack of progress in the investigation."

Angie also called insurance agent Marracino again, claiming she received a strange call at the midnight hour. "It was a scary call from one of my husband's students. They said he was poisoned."

Marracino said the topic of murder sent a chill down his spine. He reported the weird conversation to Steinwand who took notes and waited for Angie to make her next move.

On October 19, Angie called Holmes and asked why the man whom she believed killed Frank hadn't been arrested.

Knowing Angie might say something stupid, Holmes hooked up a tape recorder and called her back.

Angie was on a roll. Something had to be done, she said.

"Tell me what happened," Holmes began.

"This morning when I was—"

"Wait. Let me write this down," Holmes said into the tape recorder. "Let me write down today's date. I've been writing it all day 10, 19, 00. Go ahead.

Angie picked up where she left off.

"Okay it was maybe five or ten after eight, and I would get this call and it was call—it was blocked, caller ID blocked, and, uhm, they said—they said they wanted to tell me what was going on because they had a lot of respect for Frank, but they couldn't tell me. And I said, 'Well I won't say anything.' And they said, 'No you need to know I had a conversation with Peter' which was, he had said that the detectives came out to talk to him, but they got nothing, because if they do try and track down, they can't pin me because and they said—"

Holmes zeroed in on the phraseology.

"They can't pin me?"

Angie parroted.

"They can't pin me."

Holmes needed further clarification.

"This is what Peter is saying?"

Angie answered yes.

"To this person."

Now it was clear.

"Okay," Holmes said.

"And he said, it started breaking up, and all I heard was, 'ask them about antifreeze.'"

Holmes took notes.

"Interesting. OK. So you got a phone call about eight o'clock this morning? What race was this person? Could you tell?"

Angie said she didn't know. She knew it was a man who didn't speak with a very deep voice. She explained to Holmes that she didn't hear much. The line was static, and she was driving through the rolling hills of Paso Robles, which made it more difficult to understand.

"So he's saying that he talked to Peter, and Peter said to check antifreeze?" Holmes asked.

"No," Angie said. "He said something about antifreeze."

Holmes wanted to know if that's how Frank was poisoned.

"That's my assumption," Angie said. "That's why they mentioned it. Because. He was talking about I guess your conversation with him and that he couldn't be pinned."

Throughout the mysterious phone call, Angie told the detective she tried to recognize the person's voice on the other end of the line.

"But like I said it there was too much static, it was really, I was struggling to hear the words that they were saying."

Holmes wanted to know how the caller got Angie's cell number.

"My guess is 'cause I forwarded my phone number to my cell phone," she said.

Okay then, how did they get your old phone number?

Holmes wanted to know.

Angie had no answer, and Holmes went on to explain that he wanted to somehow track the call back to Peter, Frank's coworker. He turned back to the questions of antifreeze and who the tipster might have been.

Angie was insistent. She didn't know.

"I kept saying, you know, 'Tell me who you are. I promise that I won't mention it to anybody except, you know, maybe the detectives. You know if you want to remain anonymous until all this goes on ... that's fine.' He—they—said. 'No, you know how Peter is. I can't say who I am.'"

Angie said she thought the caller's intentions were noble.

"I think basically they wanted to—it sounds like they wanted to just tip off and give whatever information they could."

She finished her tale with a question.

"Does that help? You think?"

Holmes said, "You bet."

Angie stayed focused on the call.

"It sounds like he's not the first one that knows that Holloway is capable of this. Otherwise ..."

"I wish I could find out who that is," Holmes said. "If you get another call like that, please call us again. Try to give those people my number to call."

Angie also needed to know who was going to pay her Montebello landlord for the carpet that was ripped up during the investigation of Frank's death.

Holmes assured her Los Angeles County would cover the loss, provided the proper paperwork was completed by the landlord. She also needed assurances she wouldn't get dinged for it.

Holmes wanted more details about the phone call.

"Antifreeze tastes funny I would think," he said.

"I don't know," Angie replied.

Holmes explained he and Steinwand had been in contact with Mickey Maraccino and asked for some of Frank's medical records for reference in the county's file on the case.

Angie said the anonymous phone call scared her. She wanted to know if the new information would lead the coroner to perform more toxicology tests.

"I don't know if they've tested for that or not," Angie added.

The information Angie got from the alleged anonymous caller was crucial to making a case. Holmes knew it. Angie just thought it would put money in her pocket. Holmes was at the point where he believed the information would put Angie in jail. He didn't give up his elation at receiving the news.

"They have not tested for that. But like I was telling you, once they have an idea of what type of poison, then you can test for that particular poison. If you don't have that, you can't. There's no way."

Angie said she would call her cell company to see if she could get more information on the caller. Holmes planned to do the same thing—with a warrant. He didn't mention it to Angie.

Holmes explained some of the intricacies of phone bills and told Angie it was unlikely she would get the blocked number, but that if they gave the number to her, to let him know.

Bizarrely, Angie then promised to write something down and stick it in the mail.

The call ended. She was again the last one to say good-bye.

Angie upped the ante by embellishing her lies about Frank's coworker with more lies. As any veteran of true crime TV could have told her, it's never a good idea to lie to a homicide detective. They have ways to check out your story.

And lies about phone calls are the easiest of all to check out. At this point in her relationship with Steinwand and Holmes, just about everything that came out of Angie's mouth was a lie. Steinwand and Holmes knew they were dealing with a master manipulator.

"She knew how and when to turn on the charm," Steinwand said.

Thinking back on what he heard about Frank from his friends on the Central Coast, Steinwand said he might have been friends with the victim. But he could also see how Frank got worked.

"She knew how to suck him in," Steinwand said. "He probably really loved kids. She had this beautiful daughter. She said everything he wanted to hear."

"He was a good guy looking for love," he added. "I could tell that he got along so well with Angie's daughter too. It was pretty clear to us that she just used him to get money. "

Paso Robles

Palmira Gorham and Angie had been friends since they met at beauty school in Paso Robles. Gorham looked up to Angie. Her older friend had been in the service, she'd been married, she had kids, and she knew a thing or two about men.

Like most friendships, Angie and Palmira had their ups and downs. Sometimes they'd talk, other times they would avoid each other. Sometimes their arguments were about men, sometimes about money.

Both women felt just fine in confiding in one another. In fact, after meeting Frank, Angie told her friend about her new lover and how the two were going to move down to LA.

Later Angie would tell her friend how much Frank annoyed her, and even later she would confide in Palmira about just how much she wanted to kill him.

Palmira also hooked Angie up with her nephew, Daniel. Angie told Daniel she wanted to be with him, and explained that she would go as far as killing Frank to do it.

A couple of weeks after Frank's death, Angie took her daughter and moved up to Paso Robles. Palmira began to notice that she was spending a lot of time on the phone with detectives, the insurance company, and the coroner.

It was like the old game of telephone. Angie would call the coroner, get some information; call the detectives, try to fish something out of them; call the insurance company, try to cajole a check; and start all over again.

Palmira thought all that telephone time was exhausting.

Angie looked at it as work. She was doing what she could to outsmart a whole lot of people, and it would require keeping her story straight, figuring out what the cops knew, and trying to push the coroner to do his work.

She needed the dough, and Angie was talking a ton of shit about how much money she was going to get as soon as they figured out how Frank died. It was constant.

She even suggested he might have been killed with a combination of antifreeze and oleander. If that didn't set the balls rolling, then she'd tweak the story one way or another to suit her audience.

The cops weren't doing enough. The coroners were idiots. The damn insurance people were cheapskates. Angie needed someone to see things her way and if they didn't get there eventually she was going to help them do it.

But while Angie thought she was calling the tune, it was her that was getting played. Investigators needed time to pull all the pieces together. Even though Palmira and Daniel met Steinwand and Holmes, they didn't tell the detectives that Angie had talked about killing Frank. Privately Palmira suspected Angie had something to do with his demise.

Steinwand and Holmes had enough puzzle pieces to go after Angelina full bore, but they didn't have enough to hook her up. They needed her to boast some more, and they needed her to keep slipping.

And—just like Angie—they needed the coroner to figure out how the hell Frank actually died.

Steinwand and Holmes turned to Dan Anderson, supervising criminalist at the Los Angeles County coroner's office, with the details Angie supplied.

Anderson said that the results of the initial tests on Frank's body had been negative except for the presence of Vicodin. The blood level of its byproducts was one he considered therapeutic.

"That created a problem, because when checking for the presence of drugs, one must look for something specific. There is no general toxicology test for everything. If a test for the most common drugs is negative, trying to determine what might be present is like 'looking for a needle in a haystack,'" he said. "For example, one must look specifically for oleander toxin in order to find it."

After Angie began talking to Steinwand and Holmes about antifreeze, Anderson realized there might be something to go on. Frank's tissue samples were examined for ethylene glycol, the main component of antifreeze and the "sweet tasting" chemical that Angie learned about from Palmira's boyfriend.

Fourteen years later, Steinwand believes the original toxicology test should have turned up antifreeze, but he thinks somebody missed something somewhere.

"Things happen for a reason" the detective said.

Dr. Richard Clark, a toxicologist from the University of California, San Diego, said antifreeze could be very easily mixed into a glass of sports drink and the person who drank the concoction would have no idea he or she was being poisoned.

Oleander, Clark said, also could be mixed into a tea or with another liquid and sweetened with honey or sugar to disguise its bitter taste and then served to an unwitting patient.

Dr. Clark said that after reviewing the autopsy and toxicology test results, he believed that Frank died because he was poisoned. Blood samples showed that Frank had five to seven times the amount of poison in his bloodstream that was "needed to kill."

"Frank got the fatal dose within twenty-four hours before his death and 'most likely' within six to seven hours," Clark said.

After reviewing records from Frank's September 7 visit to the hospital in Baldwin Park, Dr. Clark said "that Frank could not have had in his system at that time the ethylene glycol that his body later contained. Frank's symptoms at that visit were consistent with oleander poisoning," he added.

Clark noted it would be "hard to say whether or not oleander played a role in Frank's death, although it could have played a part."

Clark was convinced that Frank must have had some poisonous tea laced with deadly oleander within twenty-four hours of his untimely death.

When oleander didn't kill Frank fast enough, his killer turned to antifreeze, and used lots of it.

Dr. Ogbonna Chinwah, who had performed the original inconclusive autopsy, testified that he later reexamined the body and found evidence of ethylene glycol in the kidneys. In his opinion, Frank died of ethylene glycol and oleander poisoning.

While the testing and debating about poison continued, the investigation stalled. The holidays were around the corner, and the wheels of justice slowed for a bit while investigators caught their breath.

Behind the scenes, Midland Insurance was getting nervous. When a policy goes past thirty days without being paid out, the pay-off begins to accrue daily interest. Officials from the company came close to cutting a check. Steinwand told them to hold off; something wasn't right.

A couple of weeks after Thanksgiving, investigators had their answers. It was as they suspected. Frank was poisoned. Steinwand and Holmes went back to work. In a December 12, 2000, conversation with Angelina, they began to pin down a timeline.

Little by little Angie's story began to crumble. Holmes and Steinwand first focused on Frank's last visit to Angel

Gate. They implied to Angelina that in order for him to be poisoned it would take planning.

"Who knew he was coming up there?" Holmes asked.

Steinwand completed the thought.

"Because it would take a little bit of planning."

Single-word Angie had reappeared.

"Right," she replied.

"So that's what we're trying to establish," Steinwand explained. "... Is how they would've known Frank was coming up here."

Angie rolled her eyes and walked the detectives through the process for the umpteenth time.

"The normal procedure," she said, "was that a fax would come up from LA saying these are the teachers coming."

Steinwand and Holmes took notes. They were setting Angie up. The lies were getting harder and harder to keep straight. Holmes asked about that letter she promised to send in October.

Angie began to stumble.

The conversation turned to the mysterious phone call Angie reported a month or so earlier. Holmes asked her to run through it one more time.

"It was first thing in the morning. It was like eight. I just dropped off my daughter at school, so it was probably 8:15, 8:10 something like that."

Steinwand wanted to know if Angie was in Paso Robles or LA.

"I'm up here," she said. "And, I don't remember the exact date, I have to look at the letter you know, uh—I can't remember the specific date I talked to you, so we might have it."

Steinwand and Holmes feigned interest in the letter they knew didn't exist. Without prompting, Angelina returned to describing the threatening phone call. Her New York accent was suddenly quite prominent.

"Uhm, I get a phone call, and they're like, 'Angelina' I says, 'Yeah.' She goes—he goes, 'I can't tell you who this is.'

"'Why not?' I say. 'What do you mean you can' tell me who this is?' Now I'm thinkin' prank phone call.

"He says, uh, 'I just thought you need to know something.' And I said, 'What?' And he wasn't coming clear. I was up in the hills [on] my cellphone, and they said—I said, 'Who is this? Please tell me, I promise you if I tell the detectives they won't use your name, I promise you that.' 'No, I can't tell you.'

"He said, 'I had a conversation with Peter,' and he said it was just in passing. It was like he says, he was laughing because he says, 'They can never pin it on me 'cause I used antifreeze.'"

Joe Bob let out a low whistle.

"Ooooh."

Angelina went right back to her New York-accented narrative.

"And I said, 'Oh my God, please tell me who this is.' 'No I can't,' and either they hung up or I got off 'cause it was in the hills with the cell phone."

Holmes wanted to know if Angie thought she knew the mystery caller's name.

"When he says 'I can't,' is this a person that knows you, you think?" Joe Bob asked. "I mean saying I can't or you know what I mean—"

Angie cut him off and gave up a theory of her own. She was doing everything she could to throw Peter under the bus. She implied that Peter would kill again to avoid getting caught for Frank's murder.

"I well—obvi—what I drew from as a conclusion from that was, he had a conversation with Peter, and if Peter was so open to talking to this person, then obviously if he found out this person said something you know—they seemed very close. So if knows how Peter is, he's not going to want to mess with him."

Holmes switched up and went back to the timeline. He wanted to make sure Angelina was telling him that Frank was sick after visiting Angel Gate.

She dwelled on the call and admitted that Frank spent his final days alone with her and in her care.

Holmes and Steinwand had enough of Angie's lies and her bullshit. If it was never clear before, it was clear now, no one at Angel Gate had anything to do with Frank's death.

Angelina poisoned him. She was a greedy bitch who wanted to cash in on the untimely death of her husband. Angie might have got away with it, but greed blinded her.

Now they were going to play her. After getting off the line with Angie, Steinwand called Peter.

The detective patiently explained that he needed Peter to call Angie and confront her. He needed to ask her why she was implicating him for killing Frank. He needed to ask her why she would do something like that. He needed to do it without arguing with her or turning the conversation into something that couldn't be used in court.

Steinwand asked Peter if he would follow the script, and Peter agreed.

Now it was time to pull the trigger. Steinwand set up a three-way. He and Holmes listened in from their office in Commerce, just a couple of miles southwest of Montebello, where Frank died.

Peter needed to go over the ground rules one more time.

"Exactly what would you like me to say?"

Steinwand walked him through the script.

"Basically at the beginning we'd like to—you ask her— uh—simply and in a cordial voice, why that she's told the police and why she thinks that, you know, you poisoned Frank, because Frank as you said is your good—was your good friend. Correct?"

Steinwand wanted to make sure Peter mentioned the antifreeze.

"Just see if she says anything. If she hangs up, she hangs up. Uh, if she wants to continue with the conversation, please do so."

There were other rules and planned responses. Steinwand, although new to homicide, had done these sorts of calls routinely as a gang investigator. They had a tendency to go sideways, but Peter seemed eager and willing to stay on point.

"As far as how you got the phone number, it's you know like we talked about, you know, how, you know, either from work or whatever, how you got her phone number."

The two men wrapped up their call. Peter was ready to call Angie.

He called down to homicide, Steinwand turned on the recorder. On cue, Angelina picked up.

"Hello?"

"Angelina?"

"Yes."

Peter got right to the point.

"Why did you tell the police that I poisoned Frank with antifreeze?"

Angie played dumb.

"Who is this?"

"This is Peter. Angelina you know that Frank was a friend of mine."

Angie got cold.

"No. I don't know that," she answered.

"When did I have contact with him to poison him?" Peter asked.

Angie interrupted. She said she couldn't talk.

Peter continued.

"I mean, I just—what did I ever? I just don't understand why you would say that I was—that I poisoned Frank. I don't understand that."

Angie's tone changed. She got mad at Peter and the New York came out.

"You know what? I'm not talkin' to you because that's— you need to talk to the investigator."

Peter, a military man who had a lot riding on his reputation, explained that he was braced last night. Steinwand and Holmes told him that Angie believed he was the one who poisoned Frank. He was stunned to hear it. He wanted answers.

Angie wanted to know how he got her phone number.

Peter stumbled in response. He strayed off script and kept pressing.

"I'm worried about why you told them that I killed Frank, Angelina. I—I just don't understand this. Why would I want to kill Frank?

Angie asked again about her number.

Finally Peter remembered what to say.

"I had a number for you in Los Angeles. When I called that number, it gave this number. I mean are you even gonna let me know why? I mean, it—this could ruin my life. I mean are—aren't you even going—going to talk to me about this now?"

Listening in, Steinwand whispered to Holmes.

"I'll bet she calls us thirty seconds after this call ends."

Angie continued to attack Peter. She said evidence pointed to him as Frank's killer. It was her who put it together for the homicide detectives just like a female James Rockford, private eye, or NYPD Detective Lt. Theo Kojak would have done.

"Everything is pointing that way, and that's what I told the investigators," she said.

Peter continued to tell Angelina she was no super sleuth. In fact, he told her, she had the wrong guy.

Peter pressed his point.

"Well, okay. Everything's pointing to me, okay? I mean that's just—that—that's just what I don't understand, Angelina. I mean, I never did anything to you. I mean, when you started to work at Angel Gate, I was the one that helped you. I was the one that got you the application. I'm the one that took the pictures for you. I did everything I could to help you. And then now—now you're saying that—that I killed Frank."

Angelina went cold.

"You know, I don't know why you even think that you and Frank were friends, when you know, you flat out came out and threatened him before we left. That's not friends. You need to stop and think about that, you know. And that's all I'm going to discuss with you."

Peter defended himself.

"I had nothing against Frank. I never had anything bad—and I never had anything bad to say about you."

Angie called Peter a liar.

"That's such a crock. That is such a crock. Because right before we left, you did it in front of everybody. And you had nothing good to say when we left. You need to talk to the investigator. I'm not gonna discuss this anymore with you."

Peter was disheartened.

"I just don't understand what I did. My main thing, Angelina, is just trying to figure out why in the world you would point to me as the person that killed Frank."

For a change, Angie was first off the line.

"I'm ending the conversation."

She abruptly hung up.

Steinwand's prediction was off by fifteen seconds or so. Angie was slow. It took her forty-five seconds—not thirty— to get a hold of the homicide detectives.

She sent a page to Holmes: 911.

Joe Bob called her up right away.

They exchanged short pleasantries. When Holmes asked how she was doing, Angie said, "I'm not doing well. I just got a call from Peter. He says, 'How can you say that I killed Frank with antifreeze?' and he says 'I wouldn't go spreading these things or else.' And I'm like, 'What are you talking about?' I said, 'I don't need to be talking to you.' And he says, 'Well, they'll never be able to catch me anyway,' but he says, you know, 'You just—gotta watch your back.'"

Holmes was taking notes. He gave his partner a thumbs-up. Both of them knew where their case was going and that was in the right direction. He egged her on.

"He said, 'They'll never be able to catch me anyway'?" Holmes asked with an air of concern in his voice.

"Yes," Angie answered. "And he says, you know, 'You better watch where you're going and da, da, da.' And I was just like, I—I—I'm flippin' out."

Holmes jumped in again. He was toying with Angie the way a cat messes with a small lizard or mouse before snapping its neck and delivering the dead carcass to the doorstep as a proud present for the animal's owner.

"Oh wait. He threatened you? What did he say specifically? I need to get it specifically."

Angie took the bait, not knowing she was trapped in the web of lies about Peter's involvement in Frank's death.

"He said that, 'You need to be watchin' yourself.' That I need to be watchin' myself. That's what he said. … He says, you know, 'You shouldn't have said anything,' and, I mean just his tone of voice."

Holmes continued to play with Angie. She was digging

herself a deeper and deeper hole. Holmes's responses led Angie to believe he too had been burned by that no good Peter. They were kin now on a mission to avenge Frank's death. He played up Angie's abilities as a PI working a tough case that might have stymied Kojak or Rockford.

"I'll be darned. I'll be darned," Holmes said. "Well, we—that happened. We went over there last night, and we told him and us, he's worried. He's worried. He is worried. See, what else did he say?"

Angie's response was a garbled mixture of truth and fiction. She played up her abilities as a detective and tried to help Holmes close a cell door on Peter.

"He said, well, you know, 'How can you say that—that I did this at first?' And then I said, 'You know what?' I says, "You and—you have too much of a history with Frank. And he goes, 'Well, I know that, but, they don't know that. And, they don't know that what, you know, what they can do and what they can't do, and they can't get on me because I have nothing.' He didn't say he did it. He said I better watch my back and that they can't get him."

Angie said she was worried for her safety. She said Peter wouldn't tell her how he got her number and went back and forth between caring about and not caring about it.

"But, the fact that he—he used it. And, I am flippin' out. I'm by myself—"

Holmes offered some reassurance and explained what move he and Steinwand would make next.

"What we'll do is, is we'll talk to him again. And, we're going to confront him with this. And we're going to tell him, 'Hey, look,' you know what I mean?"

Angie wanted to make sure Peter would leave her alone. She believed she had convinced Holmes and Steinwand that Peter was a crazed killer bent on shutting her up if he needed to.

"Will he leave me alone?" she asked.

She got some more reassurance—or misdirection—a little something to help her sleep better at night. She could never suspect she was the main suspect.

"Peter is going to leave you alone. No phone calls, or that's it, or [he's] going to jail right now. We'll put it right in his ballpark. It's okay, okay? That's okay, you're okay. Can you think of anything else he said? It's very important."

Angie reiterated a few points. She was told to watch her back and Peter promised her he would never be caught for killing Frank.

"Oh, oh man. I got news for him," Holmes spoke to her now as if she was an equal partner in the investigation.

Angie changed the subject and explained how she was considering joining a crime victim's assistance program offered in Santa Barbara County. She was hoping they might offer her some monetary assistance.

It played to type. Holmes and Steinwand had backgrounded her. They knew Angie had some "slip and fall" lawsuits in her background. They knew she was greedy and looking for any cash she could get her hands on, even if it came from legitimate victims of violent crimes.

Ever the helpful junior detective, Angie also wanted to discuss with Holmes how he approached Peter, so that she might understand how he decided to call her.

"Obviously you said something that alarmed him," Angie scolded.

Holmes went into an explanation that was complete nonsense. "It was confrontational. We told him exactly what we were doing, he denied it. He said, 'No, that's not true.'"

"But what he just told you is very important. Very important. And we're going to be coming back up there again. It—it'll be a drive, but we'll be back up. And we gotta talk to him again. I don't wanna talk to him on the phone.

I—I wanna talk, but I'll call you, okay? We might come up there tonight or tomorrow morning. We don't know yet. Don't worry. Everything will be okay, okay?"

Their case, now coming together, meant Holmes and Steinwand needed to meet with their captain and possibly clue in prosecutor Douglas Sortino, who would be filing the actual charges in the case.

As they stood in the office of Capt. Frank Merriman, Holmes pager buzzed. It was Angie again. She had been burning up the phone lines and called Joe Muto over at the coroner's office to see if the toxicology report was ready.

Steinwand said he'd call her. As always Angie needed a favor. And now that she believed she was a partner in the mission to arrest Frank's killer, she hoped Muto could tell her about the toxicology reports.

Angie's first question went to the matter: Did Steinwand or Holmes know what the coroner found?

"The only thing we know of is the antifreeze and just, you know, like Tylenol and stuff like that," Steinwand said. "What did he tell you?"

"Oh he wouldn't tell me," Angelina replied.

Steinwand faked concern.

"Wouldn't tell you? He asked. "Wouldn't tell you what? Maybe they don't know that they're supposed to release that to other than investigators."

Angie said she had no clue why criminalist Joe Muto declined to speak with her.

"That's why I was calling you guys," she said. "It's good to have some knowledge."

Steinwand promised to call Muto and get back to Angie with more detailed results.

"If you can get any information," said Angie, "that would be good."

After the two said their good-byes, Steinwand flipped

the tape in his recorder. He waited seven minutes then called back.

"Hi I called over there and talked to Joe Muto and he said that, 'We're not supposed to release any information on any cases to anybody but the investigators,' and I said, 'Okay. That's what I figured.' But he said they did find just typical stuff like Benadryl-type stuff or Ibuprofen."

Angie held her breath. She let out a sigh and said, "Oh. Okay."

She wanted Peter prosecuted and asked how that would take place.

"At what point, information wise, do you get to the point where you can say, 'Okay, we can go ahead and charge him' and actually make this official?"

Steinwand patiently explained the process of working through what was becoming a complex investigation.

"That's hard to determine. Believe me. It's official now. But as far as official charges, you know, no. ... A lot of our cases, a lot of times, something just pops up right in the middle, we get a phone call, you know, and someone says, 'Hey, I wanna tell you something,' or—well kind of like that phone call you got, you know."

Steinwand continued. "You know, that's—I'll tell you what. That's nine times out of ten, if we're in the middle of the investigation and we know, if we know, an informant calls, or something like—especially our gang cases or anything like that. But in this case, uh, we won't be able to make any major moves probably until we know if there's anything else—we close all the doors and you know we gotta prove that now that he, you know, had the present ability to do this."

As Angie fired off the occasional single syllable response, Steinwand continued to explain the status of the investigation and what her role—as junior detective—could be in it. Some of what was left was figuring out how Angie's suspect Peter knew Frank was coming to Angel Gate when he did.

"See we don't have anybody to tell us … how he had the knowledge to prepare … I know it doesn't take long to find some antifreeze probably and, I don't know how Angel Gate exactly is set up. And we'll—we'll be up there investigating that even more. … We have nobody that knows Frank was coming up there. We're still waiting for some records and so. But, there's … nothing that says it … that Frank was comin' up."

Angie continued to listen. She offered no suggestions or solutions.

"There's a lot of people we have to talk to," Steinwand continued. "I mean, that's kind of a big hurdle we got right now, and that's gonna be a good defense for him as far as that goes is, 'Come on, I didn't know he was coming up.' I mean, 'How am I, what? I just keep a bottle of antifreeze in my drawer?' You know?"

"We gotta show that he was ready for this. This isn't somethin' that he could've just pulled out of his hat. That's one of the big obstacles we're havin' right now. Is trying to do that. But, you know, we're gonna have to prove that he had the ability to carry this act out. And that's—it's going to be tough. It really is."

A dejected Angie said a hurried good-bye and hung up the phone.

A week later Angie was on the phone with Holmes. She wanted answers. The insurance still hadn't been paid out. Christmas was coming. She had rent to pay, presents to buy, and a life to get on with now that Frank had been dead for several weeks.

"Have you found a link yet?" she asked.

"Between?" Holmes replied.

"Him knowing," Angie said referring to Peter, the man

she wanted detectives to believe had killed Frank.

"Knowing?" Holmes asked back.

"That Frank would have been up there," she said.

Holmes knew where she was going, but played his role as the hick cop to a T.

"Oh, that Frank was up there? No. No I have not found a link yet. I mean how do you do it, you know? I mean unless he tells us, you know."

Angie fed Holmes some insider knowledge.

"Well I know there's faxes somewhere. There's, you know, there's always knowledge that someone was coming down."

Holmes played it as if a light bulb had gone off above his head, but he also explained that a fax might not be available.

"See, Frank could have called them," Holmes told Angie. "Because Frank knew—you mentioned that Frank knew a month ahead of time that he was going there."

Junior detective Angie came up with another explanation, the schedule. Frank was scheduled to go to Angel Gate in October. That meant Peter had to have knowledge that Frank was on his way there at some point, she deduced.

"I'm trying to, you know, rack my brain too, as to, okay, who would have told him. Who's trying to cover their butts saying they knew but didn't know. You know what I mean? Believe me, I'm like, maybe keeping myself busy in the wrong place."

Holmes offered some reassurance.

"We're going to pursue Peter very, very hard now. So we're probably going to be coming up there. When we come up, I'm gonna give you a call."

Holmes ended the conversation with a promise to head up the coast to dig through Angel Gate's records on his own if he had to.

Angie continued to feel she was a part of the team. She

told the detective she wanted to be there when Peter was arrested, just to see the look on his face.

When Christmas came and went and no insurance money got paid, Angie's prospects began wearing thin. Midway through January, detectives got the break they needed when a toxicology test performed at the University of California, Davis for Muto at the coroner's office found Frank had been exposed to oleander poison before he died.

Actually a lot of the testing for poison took place outside of the coroner's office. In November, when Dan Anderson, the criminalist, was first alerted to the possibility of antifreeze poisoning, he sent tissue samples to the Medtox Lab in Minnesota.

A state-of-the-art lab located in St. Paul, Medtox does critical chemical analysis for police departments around the country.

The test results, which became available just before Christmas, showed there was a fatal amount of ethylene glycol in Frank's blood at the time he died. Anderson ran tests of his own on blood from Frank's heart, his femoral blood, and on stomach and eye fluids.

He found antifreeze everywhere. In fact, Frank was dripping with the stuff.

Confirmation in hand, Anderson sent out similar samples to Birgit Puschner, a toxicologist at UC Davis.

After examining a blood sample, stomach contents, and a liver sample, Puschner found Frank had been exposed to oleander. Dr. Richard Clark at UC San Diego's poison center explained to Holmes and Steinwand how antifreeze kills.

"It's sweet tasting," he said, before outlining the three phases of its toxicity.

At first, persons poisoned by antifreeze act like drunks, he said, but after a while they begin to feel nauseous and eventually begin vomiting. Death occurs when the body starts breaking down ethylene glycol which causes crystals to form in the kidney. Within hours, victims will experience kidney failure and ultimately death.

As for Oleander, Clark told the detectives his research found it primarily affected the heart, but the poison can also irritate the stomach and could cause vomiting. Clark told the detectives that after examining the test results, it was his opinion that Frank "received fatal doses of ethylene glycol that killed him within twenty-four hours of the time of death and most likely was administered within six or seven hours of the time of death."

Clark said his opinion was based on the fact that there were very small amounts of antifreeze in Frank's stomach. That indicated to Clark it had been absorbed by the body—a process that typically takes five or six hours. Coupled with the crystals in Frank's kidney, it appeared that Frank had taken four or five shot glasses worth of antifreeze in the hours before he died.

Clark also examined the medical record from Frank's visit to the hospital emergency room. Since kidney function tests came back normal, it seemed likely that Frank hadn't been drinking antifreeze until after he left.

More likely was the possibility that Frank had been poisoned with oleander before that first visit. Whatever happened—or was going to happen—didn't happen fast enough with oleander.

"The symptoms noted at the hospital were, for the most part, consistent with oleander poisoning."

Steinwand and Holmes also began digging into Angie's phone records. It was the part of the investigation they didn't share with their junior partner.

They got a search warrant for her phone records and were pretty much able to determine that Angie never received an anonymous phone call telling her Peter was involved.

And it was that call that led them to have Frank's tissue samples retested for the presence of antifreeze. Steinwand said that before that call, neither he, nor Holmes, nor the coroner had any idea what really killed Frank. But, they all knew that when the truth came out, Angie would be involved somehow.

They also checked out Frank's scheduled visit to Angel Gate Academy. They found that an administrator made arrangements with Frank fully one week ahead of his visit. They were made directly after another teacher bowed out of the opportunity.

All the back and forth with Angie over who knew Frank was there was just that—back and forth. Holmes and Steinwand baited Angie throughout the investigation. She willingly—if unknowingly—complied.

When they needed to know the names of the poisons that were used—voila! An anonymous call arrives with the info.

When they needed to know bits and pieces about the Angel Gate operation, Angie was there to spin it to what she believed was her advantage.

It was Holmes's turn to call Angie. He told her about the oleander tests and noted it was found in Frank's body in addition to antifreeze. Now that they knew what killed Frank, Holmes said it should be no problem for Angie to get that death certificate she wanted.

As Angie saw it, that meant a payday.

Angie wanted to know about Peter. When would they be able to hook him up? He killed Frank, she said, and now they had the evidence that backed up that anonymous phone call she received way back in the fall. Holmes said unfortunately there still wasn't enough to prove Peter knew Frank was coming and therefore poisoned him

Angie said she knew there was an answer. There would be a fax with the teachers' and students' names on it in advance of the visit. Angie had worked in "admin" at Angel Gate. She knew the procedure. There just had to be proof, she told the detective. In her role as junior investigator, she would find it, she promised.

Shiny New Bracelets

Two weeks after Angie promised to help the detectives, a three-page fax appeared in the Los Angeles County Sheriff's Homicide Bureau. It was addressed to Sgt. Joe Holmes.

The seasoned veteran looked it over and made some mental notes.

No cover sheet.

Each page notes "sent by Staples #702."

There was a date and time stamp of "February 5th, 8:34 a.m."

"URGENT. Detective Holmes, I mailed this to you. Why is Peter still free? Thought maybe you did not get it. Here it is again."

Page two of the fax appeared to be a document from Angel Gate indicating there was some sort of faculty orientation on August 23, 2000.

Page three had a list of names. Frank's was there. It had been circled.

Holmes and Steinwand got together with Doug Sortino at the district attorney's office.

The play was crude. But it was what they expected. Angie had come up with crucial clues when she needed the investigation to focus on Peter. Now she was at it again, via fax.

A quick check with Staples showed that Store 702 was in Paso Robles, just blocks from where Angie was living.

It was the sort of place a chick like Angie would hang out. There was a Wal-Mart, a Mickey D's, Kohl's, and Panda Express. What else could a suburban mom ask for?

They had enough to bust Angie now. Holmes and Steinwand needed an arrest warrant and a search warrant.

Deputy D.A. Douglas Sortino arranged the paperwork. All Steinwand and Holmes had left to do was get Angie into custody. She would help them do that too.

They hit the road in the early morning hours of Wednesday, February 7. Halfway there Holmes's pager started buzzing. Of course it was Angie.

Holmes told her about the fax. He wanted to know if she had heard anything about it. Angie said no.

"Well, we're on our way to arrest Peter now," Holmes told her. In fact, he offered to swing by to pick her up so that Angie, ever the helpful sidekick like Joe Pesci in *Lethal Weapon* could be there at the moment of truth.

"Good. I want to see the expression on his face," Angie said.

Holmes and Steinwand arrived an hour or so later and knocked on Angie's door.

"I'm glad to see you," she said.

"Angelina Rodriguez, you are under arrest for the murder of your husband," Holmes said.

They read the standard Miranda rights and hooked Angelina up. She let out a sigh and promised they'd never make the charges stick. Holmes stuck around to toss the tiny squalid apartment Angie shared with her daughter and new boyfriend while Steinwand headed out to the girl's school to interview her.

Holmes pawed through Angie's purse and found a napkin with a number scrawled on it—the fax number of the Los Angeles County Sheriff's Homicide Bureau. There was a note that had figures on it including $250,000 and a final amount of $285,378. That represented the amount of Frank's insurance policy, plus the interest it had been accruing since his death. Another document listed deductions to the final amount, which included funeral expenses and bills.

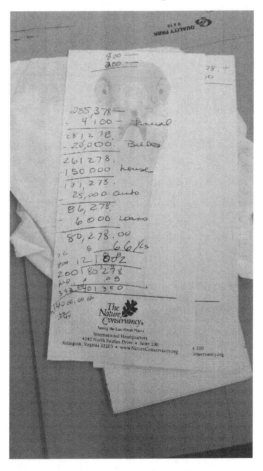

After they arrested Angie on suspicion of killing Frank, detectives found a note in her purse that detailed how she expected to spend a $250,000 insurance policy she had on the dead man. (Photo By Frank C. Girardot)

Buried deeper was a fax confirmation sheet from Staples Store 702, and the original three-page document with Frank's name written in red ink. There were also some court papers strewn about. Holmes gave them the once-over, discovering that Angie was getting ready to sue her Montebello landlord for exposing her and her daughter to asbestos poisoning. If Angie was anything, it was consistent.

Holmes, intrigued by Angie's relentless manipulative legal antics, shuffled through more of her documents. One of them caught his attention, and he took the time to read it in full.

The importance of this missive could not be exaggerated, and while it wasn't as if the Earth shifted on its axis and went careening off-kilter into outer space, the contents were enough to make the dedicated detective experience a murder mystery cliché: his blood ran cold and the hairs on his neck stood on edge.

Holmes held in his hand a letter from Barry Novak, the attorney representing Angelina and Tom in their case against Gerber. Attached was a formal report from Wolfgang Knauss, professor of aeronautics and applied mechanics at the California Institute of Technology, the respected plastics and rubber expert hired to validate Tom and Angie's assertion that Gerber was culpable in the death of their little girl.

Barry Novak never entered Professor Knauss' findings as evidence to bolster Tom and Angie's case, Novak was not obligated to share the report with Gerber, their attorneys or law enforcement.

"I bet Barry almost threw up when he read that report," commented Fred Wolfson. "I mean, there it was in black and white—one of the world's leading experts saying plain as day that that *the pacifier failed as a result of external force application; specifically, the apparent damage is consistent with someone stepping on it or rolling over it with a hard wheel.'"

In other words, while Tom was out of town, Angie allegedly broke the pacifier on purpose, shoved it down her baby's throat, and then collected on a $50K insurance policy before going after Gerber for even more money.

Holmes knew the importance of this report immediately. He'd make sure the prosecutor in Santa Barbara County got a copy of it. If Angie wasn't prosecuted for the murder of little Alicia, this report could still be used as damning evidence against Angie because both deaths—Alicia's and Frank's—were allegedly "murder for money," the coldest and most calculated form of premeditated murder.

Holmes and Steinwand were not done building their roster of potential witnesses against Angie. Holmes talked to Angie's main squeeze. Steinwand recalled him as being a pretty nice guy who struggled with drug addiction and poverty.

Way back in September, Angie told her boyfriend that she wanted to kill Frank, but now, during his interview with Holmes, the boyfriend didn't say anything, telling the cops he didn't want to get involved.

Steinwand and Holmes also talked again to Angie's best friend, Palmira Gorham, reminding her of the things that she told them before. If she would testify, she would undoubtedly be the star witness for the prosecution. Of course, if Angie knew her best friend was going to testify against her, the detectives were curious how she would react.

Twin Towers

Angie was denied bail and unceremoniously stuffed into LA's legendary and ill-reputed Twin Towers jail. The case didn't garner sufficient publicity to earn front page treatment in the *Los Angeles Times* or the lead story spot on *Eyewitness News*.

Even so, "The case was special circumstances," recalled Steinwald, "which can mean the death penalty or life in prison without parole if found guilty."

While Steinwand and Holmes returned to work, they discovered a letter postmarked in San Luis Obispo arrived while they were in Paso Robles making the arrest. The envelope contained some of the same paperwork Holmes pulled out of Angie's purse. There was also a hastily scrawled note that read: "I found this in second platoon's locker in Peter's papers. I figured this is how he knew Sergeant Rodriguez was coming to SLO, I hope this helps fry the bastard."

After examining the letter, the detectives worked with the DA, carefully considering the jury pool and how the makeup and history of Montebello impacted their perceptions, opinions, and decision making.

"The town is a place of extremes," commented Fred Wolfson. "Its south end is primarily industrial but bordered by some of the poorest neighborhoods in Southern California. Further north, where Frank and Angie briefly lived, the homes get nicer. Once you are in the Montebello Hills, the residences are positively palatial by comparison."

In many ways Montebello was seen as the immigrants' Beverly Hills. Get far enough east out of LA and you've arrived. By 2000, Montebello had become—for the most part—another of East LA's many sprawling and nondescript suburbs. The US Census noted that median household income was $38,805, and median family was $41,257. Men made more than women. About 16.3 percent of residents had a bachelor's degree. Something like 14.2 percent of Montebello's families lived below the poverty line.

Just five miles outside of LA's busy downtown and adjacent to East Los Angeles, it boasts a population of professionals and hard-working blue collar union types. It's mostly Hispanic but once was home to the nation's largest population of Armenians outside of Russia. Many of them were in the trash-hauling game.

Just outside the Quiet Cannon golf course in fact, Armenians gather annually to commemorate the genocide of 1915. A huge memorial has been erected on a hillside and every spring prayers are offered. The few survivors remaining recall the horrors of Ottoman rule in the early twentieth century.

"Montebello is also the birthplace of the Mongols Motorcycle Club," said attorney Kerrie Droban, author of several award-winning and bestselling true crime books about motorcycle gangs, including the Mongols.

"The Mongols were formed after the Vietnam War. The club got together when Mexican American vets were refused entry into the Hells Angels. Despite a huge federal indictment in 2009, the group maintains close ties to its hometown and Mongols are both feared and respected. Over the years the club has expanded into thirteen states and fourteen countries."

The town of 60,000 can claim to be the birthplace of Oscar De La Hoya, East LA's "Golden Boy."

Like all of the San Gabriel Valley, Montebello has its ups and downs when it comes to controlling crime and criminals. Occasionally tensions between rivals will flare up. Shots will be fired, and every now and again, someone dies.

The cops work the cases diligently, and homicide detectives have recorded reasonable results over the years.

A dozen and a half of these hard-working blue-collar folks, many residents of Montebello or neighboring communities like Whittier and East Los Angeles, would comprise Angie's jury. None of them would feel an ounce of sympathy for a woman who might have killed her own baby.

As Steinwand and Holmes began putting their case together for prosecutors they also considered the observations of Montebello Police Officer Sharpe, who was first on the scene. As Sharpe figured it, Angie was expensive and Frank was short on dough. She might have been sad about losing her meal ticket, but her grief seemed off—odd actually—to Sharpe.

Sharpe also remembered how she tried to put him off by suggesting that she wouldn't be surprised if Frank had been poisoned. Early on Angie didn't tell anyone she thought Frank had been given a lethal dose of something else. And when Frank visited the doctor, she didn't mention the possibility either.

Another thing Sharpe remembered: "Angie wasn't really crying all that much. I may have seen some tears, but there was a great lack of them. Everything about Angie seemed rehearsed or forced," Sharpe said. "Every now and again she would let out a whimpering sound. Although it was audible, the crying noise, there was a lack of tears,"

Insurance agent Marracino thought Angie's voicemail message the morning of Frank's death was beyond odd—in fact it was bizarre.

Maracino said that sixth sense about people he developed when he was a newspaper reporter in the 1950s and 1960s kicked in during his conversation with Angie.

"When she said, 'The coroner is doing an autopsy. They'll determine how he died,' it was cold, there was no emotion whatsoever. After I hung up with her I shook my head."

Frank's sisters also told Steinwand and Holmes they thought something was wrong with Angie's demeanor. She certainly didn't come off as a grieving widow. She barely cried, and throughout their conversations in the days following Frank's death, Angie seemed distant and cold.

Frank's sister Rebecca Perkins continued to press for answers, even after the arrest. Her gut told her something wasn't right. Something didn't add up, and she couldn't pinpoint it. Angie was squirrely. She wasn't as emotional as a grieving widow should be.

It was simply this: Perkins could smell bullshit in Angie's theory of Frank's demise.

It was during Frank's funeral when Angie tried out some of her stories on Perkins. In one instance Angie blamed Peter and then said the kids that Frank mentored didn't like her brother either. Angie explained she worked with the same kids at Angel Gate where the couple met. She left on bad terms. Everyone there knew Frank was her husband, and not appreciating the relationship, they might have tried to poison him.

None of what Angie suggested seemed legitimate, and Perkins didn't appreciate the tone of any of the conversations. Now, with the arrest, she was revisiting the strangeness of it all.

"Angie never cried. She wasn't upset. All of the bizarre information and crazy theories were delivered in a matter-of-fact tone."

Montebello cop Sharpe asked Frank's sister what she thought of Angie's stories and demeanor.

"She wasn't upset for losing her husband," Perkins replied. "She had no emotion."

Perkins had never met Angie. Never talked to her before her brother died, but her heart told her something was off. Pretty soon she would be joined in her suspicions by another sister, Shirley Coers.

Coers recalled that horrible week when the family came together to bury Frank.

Inevitably, all their conversations turned to the circumstances of Frank's untimely death. Angie laid out her theory in great detail for Coers. She accused an officer in Frank's reserve unit of attempting to poison him with bad cookies and Gatorade laced with some substance or other.

It confused Coers.

"If you wanted to poison somebody how would you go about that?" she asked Angie.

"There are many ways to get rid of somebody by poisoning them," Angie replied. "Oleander works. You can make a tea with it. It's that simple."

Coers was shocked that someone would go to such extremes to kill her brother, and after hearing the stories, she believed Angie was responsible. No one in Frank's family ate or drank any of the libations Angie prepared at a reception following the funeral.

"We didn't know what she might put in it," Coers said.

Frank's family often reflected on his short life. He'd been in the Navy and tried his hand at a variety of professional and personal pursuits including studying the law and marriage. And when he failed at both and found himself mired in an alcoholic haze, instead of falling down, Frank turned to religion and found his calling as a teacher mentoring wayward youths.

It was the divorce from his first wife that paved the way for Frank to turn to religion and move to the Central Coast in search of love. The conversion was complete. He joined a Pentecostal church. On the heels of the old-time religious conversion, Frank not only stopped drinking, he quit smoking too.

It was a fairly common biography, especially in LA—Pentecostal capital of the USA. The Pentecostal movement began in Los Angeles at a church on Azusa Street in 1906 when William Seymour, the son of slaves, traveled to a small church to preach that speaking in tongues was the ultimate path to salvation. The congregation rejected his message and promptly kicked him out.

But that wasn't the end of the story, according to an Associated Press story published in April 2006.

Committed to his belief, Seymour started his own prayer group—first at a friend's house and then at an abandoned church in northeast Los Angeles. Within weeks, people of all races were streaming to the City of Angels to see the service where worshipers fell to the ground and uttered strange, unintelligible sounds.

The boisterous, three-year revival that followed made international headlines and is widely credited as the birth of modern-day Pentecostalism. "The movement, once relegated to the theological fringe, now claims up to 600 million followers worldwide and remains one of the fastest-growing sectors of Christianity," Vinson Synan, dean of Regent University's School of Divinity and an ordained minister of the Pentecostal Holiness Church, told the AP in 2006.

Frank's membership in Word Aflame was right in line with those traditions. It was something his family knew well and respected and something Angie attempted to exploit, even after she was taken into custody.

A couple of days before her first court appearance, Angie called her boyfriend and asked him to have Detective Holmes talk to her. She had things to say. Holmes came by for a visit.

It was clear from the onset of the conversation that Angie was fishing. Maybe she wanted to cut a deal, maybe she was feeling some remorse, maybe she was trying to slip out of the death penalty. Consistent with her established pattern, Angie began the conversation with a lie.

"Frank committed suicide," said Angie.

Holmes responded by reminding her of all the lies she had told during the course of the investigation.

Angie listened. She reached across the table and turned off Holmes's tape recorder.

"What am I looking at if I tell you what really happened to Frank?" she asked.

Angie, still trying to manipulate the detectives. "Frank learned that I was getting ready to leave him, and the thought of losing his new family devastated him," Angie told Holmes. He committed suicide by drinking antifreeze. It was really that simple, she explained. Angie begged Holmes to understand her predicament, cut her loose, and right the wrong that was being done to her as a grieving widow.

Holmes said he was making no promises, got up, and let a couple of deputies take the suspected husband killer to her cell. He also didn't mention the letter about the pacifier or that her best friend, Mira, would be a witness for the prosecution. Angelina would find out about Palmira soon enough.

Thrown Under the Bus

Early on in her stay at Twin Towers, Angie learned that Palmira and her boyfriend, Carl,[8] would be key witnesses in the state's case against her. Following her arraignment, but before a preliminary hearing could take place, Angie got copies of the couple's statements and flipped out.

Her friend had to know what the stakes were. But just in case she didn't, on March 27, 2001, Angie arranged a phone call, known as a three-way, through Palmira's niece.

Three-ways are pretty common communication methods used by inmates jailed in the vast Los Angeles County custody bureaucracy. The drug dealers figured it out first. If they wanted to get a message out to a homeboy they weren't allowed to talk to, they would just call a third party and have the third party hook up a conference call. All sorts of business take place on county pay phones every day.

Shot callers and bosses can green light contract hits, settle territory disputes, handle the details of drug distribution deals, talk to their old ladies, and intimidate witnesses. All they need is proximity to a pay phone and someone on the outside willing to make the connection.

Where Angie was locked up in Twin Towers, the system had been used countless times for those reasons and more.

Angie learned the ropes almost as soon as she arrived and went right after her friend Palmira. Angie had been in about six weeks when she finally made a connection through

8 Not his real name.

144

Palmira's niece Annie Cortez.[9]

As phone time is limited Angie wasted no seconds getting down to business with her old friend.

"I wanted to know what you're planning on doing," Angie began. "Have you read your statement, Mira?"

"Have I? No," Palmira answered.

Angie took to manipulation and used the jail card as an opening.

"I don't have any remorse against you, I hope you know that," Angie said. "Okay? I mean, I considered you my sister, and I considered your kids my nieces and nephews, Okay? But my attorney sat down with me the other day and read me your statement and [your boyfriend's]. And he asked me why you're not in here with me yet. Okay?"

Palmira didn't respond with much more than a "mmm hmmm."

Angie continued.

"And I told him, let me talk to you first. Because I know what the detectives had told you. Okay? That you wouldn't be charged. These are the same detectives that told me I wasn't a suspect. They wound up arresting me. Okay?"

Palmira spoke up.

"Well I don't understand. I'm okay. If everything that they asked me, it's like, it's all an under oath thing. So—"

Angie interrupted.

"Did they read you your Miranda rights?"

Palmira was being patient, trying to figure out just exactly what the hell Angie wanted. How could Palmira be any clearer? She wasn't changing her statement to be kinder to Angie.

"You know what, Angelina, honestly, I don't know if they did or not. Because the whole thing was just kind of— it was crazy. I mean my boyfriend's dad was here visiting.

9 Not her real name.

You know, that's not exactly the greatest time for a homicide detective to come knocking at your door. You know? And I was like, fuck, this is, this is scary, you know? So I really don't know if they read me my rights or not. I can't—I don't really—I don't remember them actually doing it, but I can't say for sure that they didn't."

Angie jumped in. She had some recent experience in having her rights read to her. She knew what it was like.

"Well they probably didn't, because you would've remembered it. That's—that's the way I see it. You would've remembered them, okay?"

Palmira stayed on point.

"What I'm trying to say is, like, just in case maybe they did—who knows—if they did and I say 'Okay, fine, I'm going to retract that. I was lying.' Isn't that going to make me look worse?"

Angie turned up the concerned sister vibe and concocted a cover story for Palmira.

"There are so many people that, out of anger, would say something. And it happens all the time. People retract it all the time, okay? You could tell them that you found me with your boyfriend. I don't care. That's enough for you to snap. I know that. I know you. That would be enough for you to snap. I'm not saying it's true to you, but what I'm saying is, this is getting bigger than anybody can imagine, and it doesn't need to be. Do you see what I'm saying?"

Angie's assurances weren't enough.

"Not really," Palmira answered. "From what I've heard … it was like a death penalty thing."

"Yup," Angie answered. "And it's your statement that's gonna do that. Do you know that?"

Angie played most of her cards, but Palmira held her ground.

"It's gotta be more than that Angelina," she said. "I can

say, 'You know what? My boyfriend's sister did it.' And they're not gonna be like, 'Oh really,' you know? 'Well we're just gonna go and put her in jail,' you know?"

Angie circled around the fact she faced the death penalty and implied it was only because of Palmira's statements.

"This is why. Because it's showing that the only reason why it's considered a death penalty case is because it's showing that I thought about it before. Okay?

"And that's what your statement is saying. And it's also saying—the reason why it's gonna hurt you is because it's saying that you—when you called about the milkshake, right? That you knew what I was doing and you didn't stop me. That's where you are gonna come in. And the fact that— that I'm not—I'm not saying this that I'm gonna … please don't get me wrong. I'm just explaining it to you as it seems. Okay?

"In my file it shows the detectives writing down that you were at my house that night or the night after—whatever day you came. So it doesn't look good."

Palmira might have laughed in her friend's face. Instead she explained that if the cops were going to arrest her, they'd have done so already. They hadn't, and they probably weren't going to do it either. Angie's threats were falling on deaf ears.

"Honestly, Angelina, I have absolutely no fear of— obviously I'm going to be scared to go to jail, because that's not obviously where I belong. But I had nothing to do with this. I had nothing to do with what you did or what you didn't do. And, I don't feel responsible for it. I feel, like, betrayed that you would use a story that my mom and I were telling you to get rid of your husband. 'Cause that's what they are saying right? They're saying that you killed your husband. And they're saying that the way that you did it was the way that my mom and Carl were telling you about the lady that she either knew or that she—whatever. I don't even know."

Angelina worked in a question.

"And the way your boyfriend described dogs and hot dogs?"

Palmira continued.

"Exactly. And you're saying, or they are saying, that you killed your husband using those methods. I mean when you are talking to someone, if I say that I'm gonna, I don't know fuck—I'm gonna kill Annie the next time she leaves a dirty diaper on my floor, you know that I'm just gonna, I don't know, throw a tire iron at her, that doesn't mean that you should be, like of, you know what? Next time my babysitter does that … I'm gonna knock her in the back of the head. I feel like if you did this and the way that you did it, that maybe this was your way out. You're, like, oh, well, Mira told me the way to do it."

Angelina explained she was innocent, but would have to prove that from behind bars. She explained to her friend that is might be only a matter of time before she wound up there too.

"I didn't do this, okay? But, the way it looks, it's how I have to prove out. I have to prove it out, and that's gonna be the position that you and your boyfriend and maybe even Daniel's gonna be in. You've gotta prove it out. And you know what? I'm sitting in here, and I don't see anybody surviving in here. This is not a pretty place to be."

Palmira said she sympathized but had no plans to change her statement to Steinwand and Holmes.

"I'm sorry that you're there. But I can't—I'm not going to retract my statement and make myself look like a liar just because you think they're going to try to put me in jail, I have enough faith that this is going to be dealt with correctly."

Angie pushed harder.

"I love you guys to death. I love Daniel. But, you know

what? It doesn't look good. And they keep asking about Daniel. And they keep asking me about you and Carl."

"Who's they?" Palmira asked.

"Let's see, the district attorney, my attorney. Detectives are coming up, saying, 'You know this could be all eased up if you just talk, okay.' That's what I'm getting, Mira."

"But you have nothing to say," Palmira shot back.

Angie admitted that was right.

"I don't, but you know what? The fact that they are looking at it all is enough for me to get alerted."

Palmira wasn't biting. She was innocent and knew there was no chance she would wind up in jail with Angie as her cellmate.

"You know that my boyfriend and I had nothing to do with it. My mom had nothing to do with it. We didn't know what you were going to do. We knew that you didn't like him, you know. We knew that you weren't happy in your marriage. But that doesn't mean … I guess I just don't see it the way you see it. That they are gonna try to throw me in jail for something that I had nothing to do with. If you, the person who is, like, right, smack dab in the middle of this, knows that I had nothing to do with it, why would they—why would they be pushing it? It just seems like if they're going to do anything about it and they're gonna—the detectives or, and the district attorney and everyone, if they're gonna try to push me and my boyfriend into it, that you would be the one to be able to say, 'No, they had nothing at all to do with it.'"

Angie admitted she was looking for ways to get out from under the ordeal.

"Well I'm just saying this because my attorney is saying it to me. If it did involve other people, my sentence is reduced big time. Okay? If I am found guilty, okay? And I'm sitting in here, fighting for my life."

Palmira became indignant.

"And so, what? You're gonna throw me and my boyfriend on out just to save your ass?"

Angie's mood turned combative. She was no longer the soothing older sister and aunt, she was a calculating con facing prison time and looking for ways to intimidate a young woman with a family to raise.

"I'm not saying anything," Angie explained. "I'm saying my attorney's looking at all of it. And if he can turn around and say, 'You need to look at these people,' and there's enough for them to look at, from your words. … I wish you would get a copy of your statement and take it to an attorney. He will tell you what you're admitting to. That's why I'm calling you. Whether you're completely admitting to it or not or whatever—consciously admitting to it or not. I'm telling you what your statement says. Okay? And my attorney is not gonna sit back and let me get, you know, a full-on sentence if he can—if he can give them any kind of doubt."

Palmira went from indignant to downright pissed off.

"So that's what you are saying? You're saying that you're gonna let him do that?"

Angelina again explained her position and punctuated it with a threat.

"I'm saying that I'm looking out for my ass, and I am—I didn't admit to anything. I don't answer their questions. I don't say that, you know, that they were involved, okay? As for my attorney, it's, you know what? Yeah, we did talk about it. … I hate to say this, but Daniel's more involved than you know. Okay? But all I'm saying is, it could stop here. I'm not saying that I won't be found guilty without it. What I'm saying is, it would be a lot harder for them without it. I'm saying that it would stop anybody in your family from trying to fight for themselves. That's what I'm saying, okay? And it's really hard to sit here the last couple of days, when he told me that, and think, you know what? I don't want to see anything happen to you and your family."

Palmira was shocked. Angie was saying she would throw her, her boyfriend, and her nephew Daniel under the bus to save her own ass. It was a threat. Then, Angie got even more explicit.

"I can't say that I would've thought of these things without you."

Palmira tried to fight Angie with the logic of an innocent woman telling the truth.

"If I was just going to flip out and decide I'm going to kill my boyfriend, you know, and you told me a great knife shop to go and get a knife, I'm not going to say, 'Hey you know what? I would not have known where to get this knife if Angelina hadn't given me the reference. How dare you try to throw me and my boyfriend into this?'"

"Well, that's part of the truth," Angie responded. "That's part of the truth, Mira, and you know it is."

"Oh my God."

"You know it is."

Palmira knew a threat when she heard one. She wasn't backing down.

"You can try to throw me in this as much as you want, but, I mean, like I said, I'm not afraid because I know I had nothing to do with what—what you did. If you did it, great, you know. Wonderful. I don't care. My conscience is clear."

Palmira did slightly budge and promised to consult a lawyer. She told Angie that if the lawyer thought she should retract her statement, she would consider it.

Angie said she didn't want to get convicted and was going to do whatever it took to make sure.

"I'm not gonna be killed for something that I didn't do. You can save you. You can save your boyfriend. You can save Daniel. I told them that you were lying. You tell them that you are lying, it's gone. It's history. It's wiped out, you know, and they go by whatever else they have. I'm not saying you can save my ass completely. I'm just saying it doesn't have to get as big as it can. And if you are worried about me getting out and being with Daniel, you know what? You don't have to worry about that. I'm willing to walk away. Okay?"

Angie again admitted she was upset with the statements Palmira and Daniel had given to Steinwand and Holmes. In fact, she was mad.

"I'm coming to you. Why? Because I thought we were friends. I considered you a sister. So, you know, I don't know what else to say to you. I really don't. Nothing will happen to you by saying, "I was mad. We were mad for something totally not related. All this stuff happened after he died instead of before.' Hey, that's all you have to say. And that's how you knew about the stuff or whatever. That's it, okay?

"I know you love Daniel, but the reality is that he was my lover and that's what they look for—Hollywood, okay? I don't want it to—Mira, I'm not saying this to threaten you. I'm just saying I don't want anybody else to get hurt. And I know about your kids. Why do you think I called? 'Cause I love your kids, whether you believe it or not."

In the end, Palmira didn't budge.

"I'm not going to be drug down for something that you may have done," she told Angelina. "I'm not. You pulled my whole family into this. If you killed your husband and you still came and you were staying with my family, my sister, my nephew, my sister's husband—you were staying with all of us. You were at my house every damn day. You know it's just knowing what you did or whatever. If you did or didn't do it. Just knowing that, and then you coming here, you brought us all into it. You brought my mom, my dad, all three of my kids into it. ... Bye, Ang."

Once again the call ended with Angie being the last to

say good-bye.

Angie never heard from Palmira again. Four days after threatening Gorham, Angelina made another collect phone call to the woman's niece. In it she again explained that she needed Palmira to change her testimony.

"You know I'm putting my ass on the line even talking to [Palmira] on the phone. Even talking to you about this on the phone," Angelina said, without knowing she was being recorded. "Do you know that? I'm not even supposed to be talking to her. ... She is a witness for the prosecution."

With Palmira in the prosecutor's corner, the case against Angelina continued.

Down in the Hole

Holmes and Steinwand listened to the tapes over and over. They brought in prosecutor Douglas Sortino for a second opinion on Angie's behavior.

Sortino, a no-nonsense criminal prosecutor, made it clear he wasn't going to play games. He didn't want to lose his star witness over Angie's threats. Also, he and the detectives agreed they didn't want Angie using the telephones to arrange meetings or tamper with witnesses.

Detectives had all the information to take away Angie's telephone privileges. And, they did. To make sure it wasn't a fatal error in their case, deputies made sure Angle had plenty of time to visit with her sister, her mother, and her lawyer.

Around Christmastime, Angie tried to get her telephone privileges reinstated. She fired her attorney M.R. Ward of El Monte and asked for unlimited and unmonitored telephone access as part of an effort to sign up new counsel. It didn't work.

California felony criminal proceedings can be broken down into four distinct events. It begins with the arraignment, which means bringing the defendant before a judge, presenting the charges, and asking the defendant to enter a plea.

Angie was charged with Frank's murder and doing it for financial gain. The charge sheet made it clear that she used poison to accomplish the crime.

A second count—that of dissuading a witness by force or threat—was added to her docket after the detectives and Sortino listened to the conversation with Palmira.

The second part of the process is a preliminary hearing. In the preliminary hearing prosecutors are expected to provide a judge the skeleton of their case. After hearing the case and reviewing evidence, the judge can rule whether there is a sufficient amount of information to believe a crime has been committed.

Much of the evidence, including Palmira Gorham's statements, was presented by Steinwand. The prelim, which was expected to last two days, began on September 10, 2001.

Without belaboring the point, it's safe to say America changed forever on what was to be the second day of hearings in Angelina's criminal case, 9/11. Terrorists flew hijacked jumbo jets into the World Trade Center towers, the Pentagon, and a farmer's field in rural Pennsylvania.

The court—as did all of the country—took a day to mourn and adjust to new realities. The preliminary hearing resumed on September 12. By afternoon, Angelina was headed to trial for killing Frank and trying to dissuade Palmira.

Angie's road from grieving housewife to death penalty defendant in the high-security courtroom of Judge William Pounders on the ninth floor of the downtown Los Angeles Criminal Courts building took a detour through the punishment wing of the Twin Towers Correctional Facility.

After making threats against Palmira, Angie found herself classified K-10. Deputies sent her to the toughest part of the modern and imposing jail. She was without telephone or visiting privileges in the hole, a windowless and segregated punishment unit intended to hold the worst of the worst.

A study of inmates in the vast Los Angeles County Jail system showed the average age of women in custody hovers around thirty-five years old. Of those women, about forty percent are Latina, thirty-five percent are black, and twenty-three percent are white.

Fully ninety-one percent of women in the jail face felony charges of one sort or another. Of those, fifty percent are waiting for trial or sentencing.

As for risk factors, about eleven percent of the women waiting in the purgatory of the Los Angeles County jail are classified as high risk, which means they are a danger to themselves or others—even while in custody.

The Twin Towers facility was opened in 1997 and was designed to hold 2,200. At its peak in 2013, sheriff's officials held 4,500 inmates. Most inmates are classified as maximum security. A large number of inmates in the facility have mental health issues.

The fortified complex sits across the street from its more famous, if run-down, cousin, Men's Central. Combined, the facilities dominate a neighborhood a few blocks northeast of Downtown Los Angeles. The twelve-story Twin Towers alone occupies ten acres. Just one percent of its inmates are women.

Inside, Twin Towers looks like you might imagine a modern county jail to look. A complex of steel, concrete, and heavy Plexiglas, the cells are built in pods. The common areas and cells are visible to deputies on watch.

Angie complained about her circumstances. She cussed out the deputies and begged for long underwear. She claimed the confinement caused her to be sick. Deputies moved her to a segregated unit and gave Angie a cell of her own.

More than a year after her arrest, Angie had been through an arraignment and a preliminary hearing. By May 2002, she awaited trial in Module 211—known as the discipline module or "administrative segregation."

Los Angeles County Deputy Nick Zabokrtsky, who managed the unit, said inmates were placed there "either when the jail staff did not want them to have contact with other inmates or for disciplinary reasons." Angie hadn't broken any rules per se, she was there for "other reasons."

Making the rounds on May 9, Zabokrtsky and his partner, Deputy Rachel Jiminez, were approached by Florence Jackson,[10] an inmate who had the cell next to Angie. Florence was worried Angie wanted to kill Palmira, now a witness in the case against her. She thought the deputies might want to know about it.

In May 2002, Brian Steinwand had been on the job as an elite member of the Los Angeles County Sheriff's Homicide Bureau as a detective for nearly two years. Since Angie's arrest and near confession, his partner Joe Bob Holmes had retired and Steinwand was paired with Deputy Jeff Leslie and then Deputy Randy Seymour on a dozen murder investigations. Those cases ran solidly average. Among the cases there were victims of gunshots and stabbings. Most ended in an arrest.

Even so, when Deputy Zabokrtsky called from Twin Towers and wanted to talk, Steinwand figured it involved Angelina. He was right. Florence was terrified of Angie and had some information she thought the authorities needed to know.

A day later, he gathered a group together who met with Florence in an oversized interrogation room in the jail.

Members of the group included Zabokrtsky, Jimenez, Pat Valdez and Wayne Holston from major crimes, as well as Steinwand and his new partner Randy Seymour.

Florence had lots to tell the group, and they were all ears, even if it confirmed much of what they suspected about Angelina.

"I had a next door neighbor who told me that she was trying to create a problem for whoever she can take with her,

10 Not her real name.

and I can't just afford to be going to prison for no murders and soliciting no murders," Florence began. "I do things, but I don't solicit murders and kill people."

Steinwand looked across the table at Florence and demanded to know why she came forward. Did she think she'd get a deal on whatever crime put her in the hole at Twin Towers? Did she think she could get some money? Did she have a grudge against Angelina?

Steinwand needed answers, and Florence explained why she was telling all she knew.

"I don't wanna be involved," she said. "I don't want no involvements, period. And I realize she was serious."

In the unit where Florence and Angelina were housed, inmates are kept separated. For the most part they are not allowed to speak to one another, and they have very little contact with the outside world.

Steinwand learned that Florence was able to talk to Angelina through the pipes that connected their toilets. Florence wasn't the brightest bulb in the jail, but she knew how to communicate having been around the block once or twice.

As Florence continued her story it became apparent the relationship with Angelina didn't happen overnight. In fact, Florence only became aware of Angelina when another inmate, doing ten days in the unit for spitting on a nurse, said she was scared of Angelina and wanted to share some information.

"She didn't want the girl Rodriguez to have no information on her 'cause she was scared of her. She didn't know what she might do."

Midway through the conversation with the inmate in the cell on her left, Florence learned that Angelina was in the cell to her right. She also learned Angelina wanted to talk.

"First she was trying to talk about why I was down there

and what happened," Florence told the group of deputies. "Then she started talking about her case. Why she was there, and she kept talkin' and talkin' and talkin'. So the next door neighbor I had next to me, 'cause I was in the middle of both of 'em, would hear some of the conversation, and you know, make comments to what she was sayin' about, you know, whatever happened."

Without prompting, Angie began to spin out her life story and explained why she was in jail. Angie was frugal. Her mother was sending money, but instead of spending any of it, Angie kept it squirreled away in her inmate account. Angie told Florence that when she got out she would be buying a big piece of property up near Paso Robles.

Well into her second year in jail, Angie was dreaming of the day she would get out. She told Florence that she was going to buy a lot of things and start over. She'd have the money to buy whatever she wanted. And she explained how she ended up in county facing the death penalty on a murder beef.

"So she was telling me how her husband died and how she married him. She didn't really love him because she didn't know how to love him, and she had a hard life with different kind of men. So last night she told me exactly how he died and what she used on her husband."

Angie gave exact details because she thought Florence might help her kill somebody up in Paso Robles.

"'Cause she thinks I'm going home soon, she wants antifreeze to be used on this girl and to make it look like the boyfriend did it. That way it would throw it off."

Implication? Kill a witness, get out of jail. Make it look like someone else used the same concoction of antifreeze to kill, and of course the authorities would say, "Ah ha! We have the wrong person here."

It would have been a hugely wrongful arrest like that of

Steven Avery, the subject of Netflix's *Making a Murderer* documentary.

As Angelina talked, Florence began to take notes. She took a little nub of a pencil and carefully wrote down everything Angie said.

The top of the page had two words: "Palmira Gorham."

As the two talked through the toilet pipe, Angie couldn't see Florence taking notes. Coolly and methodically, Angie detailed for Florence how she did it.

When Florence first arrived in "The Hole" a bunch of the girls who knew her from years before at Sybil Brand shouted out her nickname and welcomed Florence back to their world. Florence admitted she was embarrassed by the return trip to county, but if the other girls thought she was some hardened gang girl that would make it easier to get along.

Florence, a tiny woman, was in jail awaiting trial for beating the shit out of her three-year-old with a shovel—a misdemeanor. She got put down into the hole on a ten-day time-out from the general population for smuggling drugs into the county jail.

Admittedly Florence, a mother of two, was tough, but not heartless. Angelina scared the living daylights out of her. She listened and took notes.

"Well, her exact words were, 'I'm gonna tell you what I used to kill my husband. You're gonna laugh. You're gonna think it's funny,'" Florence explained. "And she told me she used antifreeze."

Angie went on to explain that if Florence agreed to murder Palmira, she'd have to understand that using antifreeze isn't a quick method of killing.

"We have to give it to her and sit around for hours so she can't go call the hospital to get no help," Florence said.

Angie began to embellish her plan. She wanted to do

some staging too.

"She wanted to make it look like a robbery, and that the girl got a lot of nice furniture and computers and stuff in her house."

And, of course, whoever killed Palmira would be entitled to take her stuff. She wouldn't need it if she were dead.

Florence ran out of room on the first piece of paper and began writing on a second sheet. Angie said she was about to go on trial and needed to get rid of Palmira as soon as possible. And she was willing to pay lots to get it fixed up. A dead witness is no witness. Florence explained to Steinwand and the other deputies that she thought Angelina was playing jailhouse lawyer.

"To her, she knows exactly what's going to happen," Florence continued. "She offered me money. First she offered me $20,000. But that was to put her in a coma.

"Then she said, 'I'm going to give you $25,000.' ... 'Cause she think that I know a lot of little gang bangers and stuff like that."

Angie figured gangbangers would have no problem killing for fun.

When Florence didn't bite on the offer, Angie upped the ante a second time.

"'I'll give you $30,000'" she told Florence.

Desperately trying to get Florence's help, Angie made her final offer.

"She will buy me a house 'cause she's moving up to Arizona by her mother and the insurance money for her husband has accumulated interest," Florence said.

All Florence had to do was kill Palmira and send Angie a note that said "job well done." It would be just that easy.

Florence asked for more details, and Angie was happy to oblige. She explained how easy it is to kill someone with a sports drink laced with antifreeze.

"She did tell me that her husband had been drinking this stuff for a period of four or five days in some sports drink," Florence told the cops. "She did it 'cause he liked the sports drinks."

The best thing about feeding someone a sports drink laced with antifreeze? Lots of times the hospital can't detect it.

Florence continued to scribble, and Angie continued to talk. The two had bunks on opposite sides of the same wall. There were times when Florence couldn't hear the words perfectly. She'd ask Angie to repeat herself or spell out a word. And Angie's instructions continued over the course of several hours following the nightly bed check.

After hearing what appeared to be the beginning of a jailhouse confession, Steinwand asked Florence to sign and date her notes. She obliged.

The detective more closely examined Florence's notes, and he began to ask some questions.

"It says they call her Mira." Below that Florence printed Palmira Gorham and two phone numbers.

Another name appeared to be phonetically spelled. Below that Steinwand noticed some figures.

"You've got $25,000 and a plus with the number $5,000 below that. Okay, That's the dollar figures she was talking about?"

"Yeah" Florence said. "That's what she was going to give me."

The paper also contained directions from Los Angeles to Paso Robles, where Palmira lived with her mother and boyfriend. Steinwand read them aloud. Florence described the property as she recalled it.

"Palmira lives in the back house. There's two houses, I guess, on the property," she continued. "They both needs a lot of work done to 'em, like they falling apart and her house is the back."

The house was never locked either. It would be easy to get in.

Steinwand read through the details. Florence wrote down much of what she had just completed reciting.

Florence acknowledged Angie didn't want to kill Palmira at first. She just wanted her former friend held hostage until the trial was over. After thinking it all through, Angie changed it up. She decided kidnapping wasn't a great strategy after all.

Florence described for Steinwand how Angie talked it through.

"It'll be like tampering with a witness," the tiny inmate told the group of six deputies. "So then she said, 'Just make her unconscious.' And then she's like, 'Just kill the bitch.'"

"Those were her words?" Steinwand asked. He was a bit incredulous. After all, Angie had been so cautious before.

Florence told Steinwand that Angie didn't like being where she was and went on to say that Angie, now beginning to bloat and gain weight from a carb-loaded jail diet, explained how she ended up in the hole.

Primarily Angie believed her problems began and ended with Palmira.

Steinwand moved on. He began to examine a third piece of paper. It was a full sheet. At the top Florence wrote "The Wicked Widow."

"That's just the name I gave her," Florence told the detective. Deputies in the room smiled.

Bouncing around from topic to topic as she began to recall the conversation in some detail, Florence explained how Angie promised to pay for an attorney if there was any trouble following Palmira's murder.

At some point in the night Angie told Florence that she might want to rent a truck. There would be lots of stuff to steal. "She has nice furniture and computers," Florence wrote. "She has a lot of electronics and computers and stuff. Go with a U-Haul."

Pretty sure Angie was lying about what she wanted—or embellishing the truth—Florence took more detailed notes.

"I really didn't believe her," Florence said. "But she's serious."

Her copious notes were a goldmine. It went to the heart of the case against Angie, and Steinwand wanted to know everything he could.

"I got some questions I wanna ask you," he said and began to read aloud from Florence's note.

"It says, 'Make Palmira drink a lot of it. Break her neck after giving her the antifreeze, so it can look like a robbery gone bad. So you'll have to stay with Palmira three days after she drinks it because you don't want the hospital or a physician to save her. ... Antifreeze works fast.' Is that what she told you and you took notes?"

"Mmmm-hmmm," Florence answered, as she slightly shivered before forcing herself to nod a definite yes.

Steinwand read back more. It reiterated what Florence said at the beginning. Angie was desperate to get out and willing to say anything to get it done. Florence was smart enough to know that if Angie was willing to kill one potential witness, there would be nothing to stop the Wicked Widow from having Florence killed too.

Steinwand continued to read Florence's notes.

"'When you get out, send me a birthday card saying, job well done. I'll be able to buy you a house anywhere you want.' She told you that?"

Another shiver and another nod.

Steinwand wanted to know why Florence went to all the trouble to take such detailed notes.

Quite simply Florence explained she wanted no part of

Angie or her crazy plans.

"She talkin' murder and murder for hire. You know, I watch *Court TV* and *Forensic Files* and stuff like that on TV, and I just don't—I ain't never—this just sound like a book. It's like somethin' that's really coming out of a book. You know, I been in jail before, but I ain't never been around nobody who just—I done been around people who was in jail for murder, they never just sit around and talk about the case or nothing like that."

Other inmates suspected Angie was setting Florence up to be a patsy. They told her as much. She was taking notes to save her ass.

"I just don't need this. I don't need no murder for hire or nothin' like that and things like that. 'Cause I dont even know about killing people and poisoning people and stuff like that. She's just teaching me how to go out and kill somebody and get away—well she thinks you can get away. And, I was trying to explain to her, you know, you can't get away with that kinda stuff these days, 'cause technology. … Hell, detectives can take a piece of gum and know that you done did this or did that. But she's not convinced those things can happen to her on her case."

Florence also explained how—even though Angie was in the hole—the Wicked Widow was able to smuggle letters and contraband into and out of the jail. Angie was also gunning for another woman who had been an inmate in the hole. She believed the woman was a threat and was trying to have her hurt. The woman was doing time in Chowchilla, and Angie was using some connections she had to get at her.

Florence explained to the deputies how such a plan might work.

Florence also told Steinwand and the rest of the group how she lied her teeth off when it came to talking to Angie.

"See I just moved from Las Vegas, and she thinks I live

in LA. I kinda made up an address for her because she might try to get me killed in the end."

A lot of what Florence said led Angie to believe she was a potential gang member. Why?

"I know a bunch of gangsters and a bunch of people that, uh, can get stuff done."

Angie wanted to use Florence's contacts, the way an Avon lady might try to pick up customers from the Tupperware hostess in the same neighborhood.

Pat Valdez, the detective from major crimes, wanted Florence to explain how Angie was going to pay her once Palmira was dead.

"She's going to come and see me when she gets out," Florence said. "She's nuts. I'm telling you."

Deputies kept trying to shake Florence's story. But she kept on explaining that she had no choice but to come forward.

"As long as I'm sittin'—sleepin' by her, I can't help but be involved, 'cause knock, knock, this is—that's all her conversation is about."

Given Angie's history, Steinwand wanted to be sure Florence felt safe.

"Yeah, she don't have nothin'," Florence said. "She ain't got no antifreeze to poison me. And I wouldn't eat nothin' anyway after her. I'm thinking maybe she done stuck it in the toilet."

Even though Angelina did most of the talking when she was in the cell next door, Florence did manage to get a word in edgewise.

"In the Bible they tell you that God don't forgive you for one crime. ... He don't forgive you for murder."

When Florence explained that, she noticed that Angie got "very hostile. And then she started doing her prayers."

Shortly after the Bible lesson, Steinwand ended the

interview. He thanked Florence for her help and promised to talk to her later.

As the inmate left, Steinwand and the other detectives talked. A sort of expert at wiretaps, Steinwand came up with a plan. They would mic up Florence, send her back down to the hole, and see if she could get Angelina to spill her guts.

Steinwand learned his specialty in the gang unit. He could pretty much mic up anything and get a good recording that was useable in court. He'd heard all sorts of banter among criminals and decoded all sorts of colloquialisms in his years chasing hardcore gang members. He turned to that skill here and hoped it would pay off with a confession that he could take to court sealing Angie's fate with any jury.

Within a week, Florence was back talking to the group. A couple days after that, Steinwand had a device for her to use.

Everything had to be right.

"We had these recorders where we had to replace the batteries every day, so we had to time everything right," Steinwand said later.

The rig Steinwand decided to use consisted of two microphones—a left and a right—one for Angie and one for Florence.

Florence was told to find a way to hold one up to the wall and have the other by her mouth. That way both sides of the conversation could be recorded.

"Basically we told her to hold one side to the wall where Angelina was talking," the detective said.

'You Can't Bring Nobody Back'

Rigged up with a tape recorder and two microphones, Florence Jackson, a county jail inmate doing time in the hole at LA's Twin Towers for smuggling drugs into the women's section of the jail, was ready to talk to the inmate in the cell next door.

Her neighbor, Angelina Rodriguez, was awaiting trial for murder. Cops and criminalists said Angie killed her husband with a lethal dose of oleander and antifreeze. Coroner's officials said she hoped to collect on his $250,000 life insurance policy. Prosecutors said Angelina was a candidate for the death penalty.

Publically, Angie said she was innocent.

Privately, Angie knew that if she couldn't destroy the evidence against her, she would do her best to make sure she screwed up their case. The cops and the attorneys didn't know how much she would do to get back home.

To do that she needed to enlist Florence and a band of hardcore Compton gang members to travel from the ghetto to Paso Robles wine country on California's Central Coast. There they would kill Palmira Gorham, prosecutor Doug Sortino's star witness. No witness equaled no case. No case meant Angie walked out of Twin Towers a free woman. Freedom meant collecting the 250 grand.

She promised Florence that her help eliminating Palmira would be lucrative.

Florence wanted nothing to do with the whole deal. So

here she was with a deputy-supplied tape recorder, two mics, and a mission to catch Angie offering money in exchange for a second murder. If Florence got lucky, she'd catch Angie explaining how she killed her husband.

Leaning into the cell wall Florence asked Angie if she really wanted to go through with the contract killing of Palmira. Angie wasted no time saying, yes, of course, and explaining why. She found her salvation—and an excuse for killing—in the Bible.

"You see, I have to make, have to make a choice. That's, that's my position. You know, I need to be home with my daughter, and this is the person that I would have given my life for. And you know she's cold and I keep reading in the Bible that, you know. That the enemies will die. And that's what I keep reading you know, the enemies will die. And they're not worth being on this planet. ... You know they just hurt other people, and she did this. You know. And my daughter is my life. You know what I'm saying. I've been here long enough. It's time for me to go home."

Angie worried the hired killers could be linked back to her, and Florence said don't sweat, they are pros. After that, Angie described how the house was laid out so that the band of assassins could find their target easily.

"It's not a big house," she explained. "But it's probably going to be dirty. She has clothes everywhere, and it used to drive me crazy 'cause I used to have, I used to live in like the next town over from her, right? And I had a really nice house. And, um, I had a leather sofa, a white leather sofa. Well it was a cream color. I used to give her a key to my house, so she could come in and do laundry. I'd come home, you know, I knew she'd be there. You know how I knew? There'd be banana smeared all over my couch—from her kids. I mean is that rude or what?"

Angie suggested Florence and her friends could leave the

gas on and blow the house up. She didn't care who died as long as the explosion killed Mira and her good-for-nothing boyfriend.

It was an old house. No one would suspect that it blew up for any reason other than that, Angie said. Besides, an explosion would be a good way to cover up evidence of murder.

Angie also suggested using a gun. She explained how to execute Palmira and said the gunshot could be muffled with a pillow so that no one else would hear.

Angie told Florence, "Palmira's family was basically a shady family, and it wouldn't be odd that somebody may have had dealings with to come in and kill them. Therefore a murder wouldn't look suspicious."

Florence had questions she wanted to know how killing one person, suddenly became killing two people, or the whole family.

Angie then explained to Florence why the contract might involve killing Palmira's boyfriend or her kids.

He might be there, she said. He could testify against her just as easily as Mira. Then she went on to explain that even though she was planning a double murder, she did have a nurturing side.

"If it came down to it, I would adopt their baby. That's where I'm at. That's what I was thinking. If it came down to it where, you know, they were having a hard time finding a family member or something, a good one, I would adopt her kids. That's how much I love her kids. But I don't love her anymore. Does that make sense?"

Angie explained regardless of what happened she wanted the crime scene to look as though Mira had been killed in a home-invasion robbery. She worried that the gang members Florence was lining up might be too high to pick off the good stuff from Mira's house.

"I mean, if they're not going to be high, they're going to be able to see everything that they're going to get. And how fast they can move. You see, I'm saying the computer. You have a lot of cords and all that other garbage that you have to get out, you know. Are they going to mess with that? And somebody sees them walking out with the cord? You know what I'm saying?"

Florence baited Angie.

"How are they going to get that rock off of her finger?"

Angie said it was simple.

"Just slip it off. If they want it, I'm sure they'll figure a way."

Was there more jewelry? Florence asked.

"I'm sure there's more. She's a spoiled little bitch. Spoiled little brat."

Angie said she had a domino theory for taking care of witnesses in the case against her.

"When you take care of one, the rest go," she said.

The case against Angie all came down to what Palmira might say on the stand. Namely that she heard Angelina joke about killing her husband Frank.

After that, "They got nothing," Angie told Florence.

Florence wanted just one more detail.

"I'm trying to see how you do a gas leak," she said. "Didn't you say a gas leak and a fire?"

Angie patiently explained her reasoning.

"One would cause the other," she said. And the result?

One very dead family.

"Make it look like robbery gone bad or a boyfriend gone mad," Angie said.

Florence leaned into the microphone capturing her side of the conversation and whispered.

"This bitch is crazy. Evil bitch. Shit."

Contract

Brian Steinwand, lead investigator in the homicide case, now sought the assistance of Pat Valdez and the major crimes unit.

At this point it wasn't just a murder investigation, Angie was now engaged in an active plot to kill her old friend Mira—a witness against her.

The detectives wondered, how many other inmates had she promised $30,000 to already? They began scouring witness logs and enlisted prosecutor Douglas Sortino in their cause.

With no criminal record, it was unlikely immediately after Angie's arrest that Sortino would ask for the death penalty. No one in California's history had gone to death row with a clean criminal record. What else was out there?

Steinwand scoured through public records. He examined paperwork from various court battles Angie waged through the years. There was a pattern. She was a scam artist. She pursued several slip and fall cases and turned some lucrative settlements over the years.

Upon closer examination, they all looked fake. Angie was a scam artist, and her insurance scam with Frank's policy was going to be the big score. Steinwand took a closer look at the death of Alicia Fuller, Angie's baby who choked on a pacifier. He realized it wasn't what it seemed. In fact, it was clear to him—even if it wasn't clear to authorities in Santa Barbara County, that Angie killed that baby.

Steinwand was now certain: Angie staged the crime scene and the death of her daughter. It was done for money. She'd been successful once. Why not try it again?

"I looked at the reports, and I saw how she was trying to say that her mother was a nurse and how she tried to portray herself as nurturing and caring.

"But look at what happened as emergency and fire were responding to the scene at the apartments in Lompoc. In every other case I've ever seen like that the mother stays with the child, they are not out front directing traffic the way Angie did.

"She goes out front and flags down the ambulance. She knew they needed to see the baby laying in the crib. You don't do that. You don't leave your baby. She needed them to see it up close. She needed them to see the broken pacifier. She needed them to believe something went horribly wrong."

Steinwand contacted his counterparts in Santa Barbara. They weren't particularly interested in the case, and they didn't like the idea of a cop from LA trying to big-time them. He went back through the reams of paperwork he and Joe Bob Holmes took during that first search warrant.

All the proof he needed was there. If the DA couldn't use the information to prosecute her for a second murder, prosecutor Doug Sortino could for sure use in it a death penalty hearing.

Steinwand was also certain that Angie meant to kill Palmira Gorham and would stop at nothing to get the job done. He talked over the situation with Pat Valdez, and the pair hit on a plan. What if they got Angie to believe Palmira was dead? How would she react? What would she say then? However that went, Angie's reaction needed to be captured on a video recording.

Steinwand, Valdez, and Seymour went to visit Palmira up in Paso Robles. They explained the situation. She was in danger and needed to know. To keep Angie from following through on her death threat, they needed Palmira to play dead.

A makeup artist put a bullet hole on Palmira's head. They sprinkled some pig's blood on the floor. A criminologist snapped pictures. Steinwand and Valdez planned to get the best shots in the hands of Deputy Joe Mejia.

On a ruse, they had Florence pulled from the hole. She needed to be far away from Angie once and for all. Now they needed Mejia to pose as a go-between from Florence's gang member associates and Angie. He would be the guy delivering news to Angie that the hit had gone as planned.

The photos were gruesome and appeared completely realistic. Once they were delivered to Angie, detectives knew she would believe she had eliminated the only witness against her and also knew she would believe that gave her a better chance of walking. After all, with no Palmira, there was really no case. No one else could testify that Angelina knew about oleander. For that matter, no one else could testify that Angie knew about the sweet taste of antifreeze and there was no one else who could tell a jury that Angelina hated Frank and wanted him dead.

She only said that to Palmira. Detectives knew from listening to the tape that Angie was serious. The fact that she was willing to let Palmira's young children die or that Palmira's boyfriend might also be executed was something that made even experienced detectives take pause. Steinwand, who thought he knew a lot about Angelina, really began to question what sort of monster she had become. He worried about his witness because she didn't deserve to be caught in Angie's web of lies and treachery. And he worried about Mira's boyfriend and her children for those same reasons. This was one sick killer they were dealing with, and it appeared to him and Sortino, the prosecutor, that Angie would stop at nothing to stop Palmira. He realized they needed to act soon and completely take the possibility of a jail-ordered hit on an innocent family off the table.

Detectives made it appear as if key witness Palmira Gorham had been shot to death in an execution murder designed to save Angie from prison. (Evidence Photo)

In early June, Mejia, posing as middleman Antonio Davis, and Angelina had a private visit in a room usually reserved for attorneys and their clients. Valdez and Steinwand captured the scene on videotape.

Mejia, dressed like a lawyer, waited as Angie was led into the room. A matron brought her in and slammed the door hard. Angie gave Mejia the once over. They sat across from one another separated by a Plexiglas divider. Each held a telephone receiver.

"Who are you? A lawyer?"

"No," Mejia answered. "I'm here to see you."

Angie said she was embarrassed.

"It's not a great place to look your best and all of a sudden you're seeing somebody you know."

Mejia reassured her. He let her know Florence sent him. "You look fine."

Angie complained about conditions and said she hated her life in the hole.

"I shouldn't be down here. There's no windows. There's no mirrors. That's why I'm thinking, 'Oh God I probably look like garbage.'"

Angie told Mejia she was teaching Bible studies to fellow inmates, and that helped her get through even as the cops were playing "their little games" and on "that power trip thing."

"You know what I'm thinking, 'I'm going home someday' and hopefully soon, you know."

Angie turned the conversation to Florence.

"What did she tell you about me?"

"She said you were good looking," Mejia answered.

"So you come for looks? The brain don't matter? I get it."

"It's all one package," he said.

"Oh yeah, well, it's a big package," she responded.

Angie continued with her laundry list of complaints. Her attorney never came to see her. He wasn't bothering to get her out of jail. She was frustrated by the lack of an ability to use the telephone. She explained that she wrote letters—lots of them. Her missives had gone out to California Sen. Dianne Feinstein, Gov. Gray Davis, and the ACLU. She was about to write to Judge William Pounders, too.

"I'm very professional in my letters. They can be pretty straight forward. I'm old enough to know what to say. I've been in the business world long, too."

Angie listed her jobs for Mejia.

She was a district manager for restaurants. She was in the military—both the Air Force and the National Guard.

"The Air Force is like Disneyland you know," she added. "I mean it's not like the Marines."

Mejia cut to the chase.

"You need to contact your family, because something bad has happened to one of your friends, okay?"

"What?' Angie asked.

"You need to call your family," Mejia said.

"I can't call them," Angie said.

"You need to call. Something's happened," Mejia said, holding photos of the "assassinated" Palmira Gorham up to the window.

Palmira lay face down on her bed. There was a bullet hole in her temple. Blood oozed out and onto the covers. The two photos were epic crime scene fare. The first, an establishing shot gave the overall picture of the dead body. The second, a clinical look at the head shot that took her out.

Angie gasped.

"Oh my God," she said. "Where did you get those from? Oh my God."

He held up a handwritten note.

"How do you want to take care of it? These guys are asking about the money."

Angie wrote back.

"I thought Florence stopped it."

Angie wrote several notes on a single sheet of paper that she folded so that only the lines could be read one at a time. She scribbled out a second note.

Mejia repeated his message.

"We need to know how we're going to take care of this. You understand what I'm saying?"

Angie played dumb. Maybe she forgot that she promised

Florence and her Compton connections $30,000 and a house to kill Palmira.

She kept staring at the photos.

"Oh my God. What is there to take care of?"

"You know what I'm talking about. Okay?" Mejia said.

Angie stared at Mejia. Palmira had been executed. It was exactly what she had asked Florence to do.

"Where did you get those?" she asked.

Mejia swiped the photos away.

"You see it?" he asked.

"Yeah. Oh my God. I—" Angie was at a momentary loss for words. "You know who that is, right?"

"Nope," Mejia said. He didn't care. He was just a messenger.

Angie held up a note.

"My star witness. Best friend of 6 years."

Angie tried to talk her way out of paying up right away. She said Florence knew how the deal would go down.

She quickly scribbled out another note.

"This is what I told her. When out as soon as insurance in—About 45 days I give to Florence."

She verbalized a thought.

"Oh my God," she said again. "Shit. Do you know anything about that besides that? Shit."

"No," Mejia replied. "They gave me an envelope. I was told to come here. Here I am."

Angie tried to lighten the mood.

"That's the only reason you came?" she asked. "I don't know what to say. I don't."

Mejia needed to know some things.

"What do you want me to tell them?"

Angie broke out in a cold sweat.

"Oh God. Oh God. Oh God. Oh God. Oh God. Oh God. Oh God. This is what I told her. Oh my God."

Angelina desperately tried to talk her way out of the contract. She said she didn't think Florence was serious.

Angie was a mess. First she wanted Mejia to call her mother in Arizona to get paid. Then she said she needed an attorney.

Angie went back to defending herself.

"I thought Florence was kidding," she said. "I swear to God I did."

"This is all business," Mejia replied. "I'm just here sending a message."

"What a way to start a conversation," Angie responded. "I guess you call it a blind date, huh?"

She began to shake. There were too many open ends. Angie explained she might go home now that Palmira was dead. Maybe Florence was going to go down for witness tampering, she mused. She wanted to know why Mejia was so calm.

"A man's gotta do what a man's gotta do," he said.

"But you look so innocent," she marveled.

"I am innocent," Mejia responded in his one moment of truth.

"I told you when you came in that you looked like you were a lawyer or something. I thought I had a new one. I thought somebody was coming to my rescue, you know."

Mejia tapped the envelope in his breast pocket.

"You don't need to be rescued anymore," he said.

Angie blamed Palmira for her own brutal execution and explained that even if she got out right away it would be difficult to pay for the hit on such short notice.

"This whole thing is a mess. I've lost everything being in here. I have civil suits I need to start."

Angie changed the subject and said Florence was wrong. Angie never said she wanted Palmira to be killed.

"They took pictures? You know? What is that? That

doesn't give you a sweet picture of me now, does it?

"I was kidding. Oh my God."

Angie began putting things together.

"I was wondering why they beefed up security on me now. When I walk around downstairs, I'm escorted now, and they've never done that. I am so ready to go home. You know I feel at peace with that. Do you know what I'm saying?"

Angie started complaining again. She hated the nurses. She hated the deputies. She didn't belong in the hole. She didn't even belong in jail. She wanted out and wanted to get on the first flight out of California and back to New York or Florida as soon as she was set free. She thought she might find some redemption and maybe some freedom back in the Far Rockaways. She needed to get back to the old neighborhood.

"You know, I've lived in California for twelve years, and in those twelve years my life has been one trial—one dilemma—after another and I don't know. Just here, the detectives alone turned everybody that I ever cared about against me."

She needed an attorney though. A good one.

"There's so much stuff they've done, you know? I mean if I told you it'd make you—well, I don't think it would make you sick because you've—it seems, sounds, like you've dealt with more than what I've gone through."

Mejia assured Angie.

"You're gonna get out," he said. "It's taken care of."

"I'm gonna go home," Angie said.

Mejia turned one last time to the business at hand. Would he and his partners get paid?

Angie wrote another note. She held it up to the glass.

"It's up to how long the insurance takes."

Out loud she added, "It's just a matter of my stupid attorney getting here and doing what he has to do."

She turned the conversation personal.

"Okay. Tell me how many kids you have?"

"Why do we have to talk about kids?" Mejia shot back.

The meeting was drawing to a close.

"Hey, when are you gonna come back?" Angie asked.

"How about next week?" Mejia said.

It was the end of the conversation. Steinwand and Valdez had their video. Mejia walked out. Angie left the room feeling hopeful. The next time she would see Mejia it would be in court. And he'd be wearing the uniform of a Los Angeles County Deputy Sheriff.

Deputies grabbed Angie when she walked out of the visitation.

She was searched. Deputies took her notes. She also added an entry to her address book. It read: "Antonio Davis."

Angie's address book was strictly a jailhouse affair. The handmade, neatly folded and multipage document contained all the phone numbers and addresses she could remember. It had notes on each entry and was covered with sketches and drawings that gave the palm-sized book a feminine look.

Angie was hauled back to her cell, and a towel was shoved under the entry so that no light from outside could get in. Angie spent much of the next several days dreaming up ways to get back into court and back to a telephone.

To that end, she sent an eleven-page memo to Judge William Pounders listing the abysmal conditions in the Twin Towers county jail.

She complained about being exposed to tuberculosis. She said she wasn't allowed to regularly shower. She whined that when she did bathe the deputies watched her and made sexual advances.

Being in Module 211—the hole—meant she was exposed to conditions that she was unused to, Angie explained.

There was poor lighting, cold air, too many bugs, not

enough windows. Deputies refused her access to fresh air, television, newspapers, or outdoor activities.

Angie's complaint went on about "24/7 door pounding, yelling, pepper spraying, inmate verbal fights, and lesbian sex talk." She might have been living in a real life episode of *Orange is the New Black*.

Angie said Steinwand threw her down in the hole to torment her, and it meant that she didn't get her mail.

She demanded to be transferred to the Metropolitan Detention Center or the Montebello Jail, both of which house federal prisoners. She asked for a nonbiased investigator to examine her complaints, pleaded for access to the facility's law library, and begged for a mental health evaluation.

Her motion was denied.

In the background prosecutors were preparing another case against her—this one for witness tampering. They figured that the conversation with Mejia was enough to bolster their case. It certainly made their death penalty pitch that much stronger. The team laughed every time they listened to Florence on tape. Angie was indeed an "evil bitch."

They delivered a discovery packet loaded with incriminating information to her attorney M.R. Ward. They laid the new evidence on him. He was pissed and demanded to see Judge Pounders.

Four weeks later Ward asked to be taken off her case.

Angie, he explained, couldn't be properly represented due to her "total lack of cooperation in preparation for trial and her totally uncalled for misbehavior while in jail."

Ward had visited Angie nineteen times since her arrest as well as in the lock up during her court appearances. Although he told her to keep her mouth shut, she continued to talk about her case with anyone who would listen.

Ward had a loser on his hands and wanted to rid himself of Angie before she ruined his reputation.

He got removed. Angie wanted to represent herself but got a public defender and limited phone privileges instead.

It would be another year before trial for Frank's murder could get underway. While waiting for trial, Judge Pounders ordered a psychological evaluation of Angie. He had her explain her problems in private.

Angie told Pounders she now had an eating disorder. Additionally she said she was suffering from hysteria and claustrophobia from being in the hole.

After several hearings and testimony from psychologists and deputies, Pounders decided to keep Angie right where she was. He ordered deputies to expose her to some sunlight and take her to see a psychologist whenever possible.

As the case rolled on, Pounders had an opportunity to hear Angie on several motions. She frequently disagreed with her attorney and wanted all her arguments aired in open court. She believed she was not being competently examined by psychologists. Pounders cut her off.

"Isn't this kind of a catch-22, where the person who says he or she needs psychological help is the one who's to be examined?

"And let me mention, too, the video I saw of you being interviewed or talking with the undercover officer who purportedly had carried out a contract killing on your behalf, you were intelligent, charming, lucid, and very persuasive."

It was "pretty good evidence," Pounders continued, "that you are altogether, that your mind is working very well."

Angie, now assuredly facing death, didn't like that answer.

"On the inside I'm a mess."

Despite Angie's maneuvering, her attorney David Houchin told Pounders he was ready for trial.

"My theory of representing my client has differed with her opinions and her wishes and her desires, and these are just hard decisions that I have had to make, and I'm going to make them."

Angie ran through her list of complaints one more time. She claimed she was subjected to intensifying "mental torment and vicious and despicable treatment." She claimed she was only allowed to shower once every six days, had no recreation time, her medications were manipulated, she claimed deputies often made sexual advances.

Angie also listed problems with lighting and temperature.

She said she was tired of "being housed in a dirty and toxic-smelling cell infested with mites, poisonous spiders, and fleas." She complained that she had been made to wear the same uniform and underpants for a week and the same thermals for four months at a time. She said the deputies refused her provisions when the weather got too cold.

Pounders made it clear to Angie she couldn't put off her day of reckoning.

"Obviously you are nervous about the situation," said Pounders. "Nobody going into a death penalty trial, and that includes the court as well as the attorneys and certainly a defendant who has been waiting two years for this, is anxious to see that process go forward, but two and a half years almost now, it has been a long process and it has to end as some point."

As for the conditions about which Angie constantly complained, the judge was empathetic but not sympathetic. "No one who is confined in jail for two years is going to be as normal as everyone else. The circumstances are difficult to tolerate, and in some cases oppressive, especially under your circumstances. Though as we've had the hearing on it, there are things that you apparently did that would justify the circumstances. There are tape recordings that substantiate some of the allegations made against you."

Trial began on September 29, 2003. Frank had been dead

for three years.

The jury heard from Stephen Sharpe, the Montebello police officer who first arrived at the tiny home on Marconi Street.

They heard from the doctor at Kaiser who treated Frank when he first got sick. They heard from Frank's coworkers, and they heard from Frank's sisters and his mother. They heard testimony from Angie's former boyfriend, and they listened to Palmira Gorham explain how her friendship with Angie developed and fell apart. They heard from Mira's mother and Mira's boyfriend.

Steinwand testified, so did Pat Valdez and Joe Mejia from the sheriff's department.

Jurors heard from Mickey Marracino, the insurance agent, and Dr. Fredrick Reiders, a toxicologist who explained how poisons worked.

They heard from Joe Bob Holmes, who explained how he worked his charm with Angie so that she would tell him what she poisoned Frank with. He told them that every time Angie talked about Frank, she talked about money and getting paid off by his insurance policy.

Frank's sister Rebecca Perkins told jurors that three years after her brother's death she was still struck by Angelina's cold demeanor.

"She didn't cry. She wasn't upset. She was just matter of fact. She was not indifferent. For her husband dying, she had no emotion."

Marracino made a similar observation.

Florence made an appearance as did the deputies in the jail who kept watch on Angelina since she was put in the hole at Twin Towers.

Florence didn't want to be branded a snitch. She forgot just about everything that she told deputies more than a year earlier.

She didn't recall ever meeting Angie and said she never took notes of their conversations.

Almost a month after the trial began, attorneys on both sides rested their cases on October 27, 2003.

Jurors had three counts to consider. They reflected on the photos, posters, scientific evidence, transcripts, and video recordings that they were presented.

Their first question was about Palmira. When did she become a witness and not a person of interest? After a few hours of deliberation, Juror No. 7, the foreperson, sent a note to Judge Pounders claiming jurors had deadlocked on two counts.

Later in the day Pounders got a second note.

"We have no need for additional testimony or evidence. We are still deadlocked on the special allegation of Murder for Financial Gain and Count 3—solicitation of murder. We have approached these deliberations with sincere diligence after a substantial amount of discussions. We hold a very strong belief that further deliberations on these two matters will be futile."

He told them to keep working at it.

The next day, jurors wanted to know still more about Palmira Gorham. Had she been a suspect? A witness? When did she begin cooperating with police? What made her decide to tape record her conversation with Angie? There were a lot of questions about her involvement.

Pounders got a third note from Juror No. 7

"We request the attorneys to clarify at what point Palmira Gorham became a witness. Our question relates to the timing of the March 27th, 2001, telephone conversation between Palmira Gorham and Angelina Rodriguez and whether or not Palmira was a witness at that point."

Jurors also said they would continue deliberations on all three counts, but they wanted a read back of Palmira

Gorham's testimony.

"In contrast to our request yesterday, we would like to continue deliberations on the special allegation of financial gain and count #3—solicitation of murder," Juror No. 7 wrote.

After two and a half days of deliberations, the jury came back with its verdict and found Angelina Rodriguez guilty of murder by poisoning. The special circumstance that she killed Frank for financial gain was also true. It meant she would face the death penalty.

As for the other counts? Jurors said Angelina was guilty of attempting to dissuade Palmira from testifying against her. They couldn't agree if she was willing to pay someone to have Palmira murdered.

Two weeks later the seven men and five women who agreed Angie was a killer were asked to consider the death penalty.

The death of Alicia Fuller played a key role in the two-day hearing that began on November 10. Pounders allowed jurors to hear testimony from Dr. Knauss , the expert who wrote the letter explaining that the pacifier on which the baby choked to death had been tampered with.

Now, after the intervening years between Alicia's death and Frank's, here was Dr. Knauss speaking out in the death penalty phase of Angelina's trial and essentially telling jurors that the woman who killed her husband, also killed her own baby. It wasn't too much a stretch to link that both cases were insurance murders, and detectives concluded that Angie thought she found a way to fool the system.

Murder is frowned upon by insurance companies. Angie was later sued by Gerber who sought the return of the payoff they made nearly a decade earlier.

Pounders also allowed them to hear from William Vicary, the psych doctor who said Angie had remorse about Frank's death but was unable to express it in any human way.

Vicary's testimony also opened the door to some information jurors hadn't heard—namely it was Angelina's daughter who administered some of the poisonous sports drink to her stepdad in his final hours.

When Vicary testified that he thought Angie was a wonderful mother and suited to be a parent, Sortino asked him if would change that opinion knowing that Angie directed her daughter to bring Frank some red sports drink that was laced with antifreeze.

"It's a horrible, indefensible act," he said. "However, considering all the data, this circumstance did not alter the opinion that Angelina was a loving and supportive mother."

The sentencing hearing lasted a day and a half. Deliberations took another half day. When all was said and done, the jury recommended that Angelina be sent to Chowchilla and be put to death.

One female juror told a reporter she thought the trial and penalty hearing had been "riveting." She stood by her vote. So too did Juror No. 7.

Angelina's fate rested in Pounders's hands. He set a January 12, 2004, court date for sentencing.

That night under a sky shrouded in thick fog, the wind howled, lightning cracked, and an inch of rain fell on Los Angeles.

Angie was returned to her cell. She took note of the weather and counted the days until she would be sent to state prison.

She would later say the weather was a sign from God. She claimed to have sung religious hymns through the night.

'I've Never Seen a Colder Heart'

It was one of those typical January days in Los Angeles. The sort of day folks on the East Coast can enjoy every New Year's as they watch the Rose Parade on TV.

The sun was out, the skies were clear. Palm trees swayed in a gentle breeze that blew through the canyons and mountain passes.

Angie's attorney David Houchin arrived first. He defended his client and told reporters that despite the jury's verdict, Angie didn't deserve death and was "not involved at all" in the death of her child nearly a decade earlier.

Prosecutor Douglas Sortino described Angelina as pure evil.

"She murdered her husband. She tried to frame somebody," he said recalling Angie's attempt to have Frank's friend and coworker Peter arrested for killing her husband.

It was a historic day. If Pounders sentenced Angelina to death, she would be the fifteenth woman on California's death row and the first put there without a prior criminal record. Longtime court observers knew the likelihood of Angie ever meeting the needle were slim.

The last time California put a woman to death was in 1962. That infamous inmate was Elizabeth Ann "Ma" Duncan.

Described as an overbearing and overprotective mother, Duncan hired two men to kill her pregnant daughter-in-law in 1958 then tried to cover up the crime. The cover-up was intended to be clever. She filed for an annulment posing as the dead daughter-in-law and paying a man she didn't know to pose as her son Frank for the hearing.

A series of missteps followed, and ultimately Ma Duncan was convicted of killing the wife of "mama's little boy."

After three years of appeals in the case, Duncan was executed in August of 1962. Her last words were, "Where's Frank? I'm innocent."

Angelina had tried the "I'm innocent" route. It didn't work.

She was led into court wearing a black suit, with a white blouse. Her thick and long dark hair, still wet, was pulled back and held at the crown of her head in a clip.

Tense, she rocked back and forth in her chair at the counsel table. She glanced back into the gallery once or twice hoping to catch the eye of an elderly man who sat with reporters.

Houchin made a motion asking Pounders to consider life without parole. Steinwand was asked to testify about Florence's role in the case.

He said he interviewed Angie after she told Florence she wanted to kill Palmira.

"I told her we had information, recorded information that she was trying to harm witnesses. And we had information that other inmates may have left the jail with instructions as to who to harm. I asked her to give us those names so we could stop anyone from being harmed."

Angie declined to help.

Houchin wanted to know why Pat Valdez and Steinwand videotaped Mejia's meeting with Angie where he showed her the photos of an allegedly dead Palmira Gorham.

"It was great evidence to see the reaction," Valdez said. "It was a great piece of evidence for me."

"This case was a life without parole case, after that, it was a death penalty case," he said.

An argument ensued. Houchin wanted to save his client. He wanted a new trial. He said it wasn't fair to entrap Angie with the grisly photos.

"I've never seen a case where the death penalty was dropped and reinstated as in this case, and I've been doing this for a while."

Pounders wasn't having any of Houchin's arguments. In sentencing Angie to the gas chamber, the judge pointed out Angie's reaction to the faked death of her friend.

"Evidence was presented that her best friend was killed, and her reaction was chilling," Pounders said.

Angie's alleged murder of her own daughter also weighed heavily in Pounders's ultimate decision.

"The death of Angelina's child was a significant event in the penalty phase. The testimony of paramedics responding to the scene—she's out in front of the house alone. The baby is back in the house, dead. They said this doesn't happen. The mother is always with the baby. To me, that was very persuasive evidence."

Pounders also expressed an opinion about the quality of Sortino's case and the work that Steinwand put in as an investigator.

"This case was proven not just beyond a reasonable doubt, but to an absolute certainty. There is no doubt Angelina is guilty of this."

The gallery raptly listened to Pounders as he continued. The judge had been on the bench for nearly two decades. A lot of cold-blooded killers had been before him. He'd sentenced Mexican mafia members, drug dealers, and serial killers to terms in state prison and death. If anyone knew what a murderer looked like it would be Pounders.

He went after Houchin's assertion that Angelina had

expressed some remorse to the psychiatrist.

"There has been no indication of remorse at all during this trial, and in fact it's hard to believe that there would be any remorse.

"Frank was only married for a few months when she created the circumstances under which he received $250,000 life insurance with her as the beneficiary, and two months after that roughly attempts to kill him by the use of loosening the gas connection, which also endangered not only her husband but also the community around her husband in case there had been an explosion. Then attempting to poison with oleander, and on the failure of that a week later poisoning him for a long period of time with antifreeze.

"And I have to say it's the coldest killing I've ever seen. Most of the murders and most of the murder cases in this court and over the past twenty years I've never seen a colder heart. She seemed to have no care for the agony that she put her husband through, and the sole goal being to make a profit in his death."

Angelina alternated between rolling her eyes and squirming in her chair. She whispered to Houchin and clutched a stack of papers that sat in front of her.

When Pounders was nearly finished, he was interrupted by Angie's mouthpiece.

"My client wishes to address the court," Houchin said.

Angelina looked down at the documents, which comprised the bulk of a 113-page handwritten statement. The documents sat in front of her. She spoke.

"I have very strong evidence that was not presented that would make everything look totally different in the eyes of this court," she said. "If I'm going to be convicted of a murder I believe all the evidence should be presented and it was not—including my daughter's situation. I ask for a reasonable ear to hear all of this."

She praised Jesus and turned to the media, asking reporters to record her words.

"I come before you after three years of silence, damned by this prosecution and those I call friends. Me, alone, amongst a half a dozen Caucasian males."

A statement from Angie would be nothing without a condemnation of conditions in the Twin Towers jail.

"I am unjustifiably, unlawfully housed. Worse than an animal. This is a place where a grown woman must beg for a piece of toilet paper and sanitary napkins, because more is not given. I have trusted three attorneys. Not one has defended me in my innocence.

"I was sick for months after seeing the made-up pictures of someone I cared about, having a fake gunshot wound to her head. Even I can be pushed under such conditions. In her heart of hearts Palmira knows I was true. I cannot take the full blame, but I still am sorry."

Angelina then explained how her faith was helping her through what she described as the most difficult of times. Not only was she jailed, her mother had died. Now her voice cracked. She began to cry and pinched the top of her nose.

"I prayed, and God told me to watch, listen, and wait. I am not afraid. I just don't remember a lot from those four months after Frank's death. Perhaps the pills and alcohol I took did not let me retain.

"I am a pathetic liar. Actually I am pathetic at lying. I don't make a practice of it. I did within the four months, and that's why it was so obvious. We all make mistakes, and I've made mine. But murder is not on that list.

"God knows. I know. My husband knows what is true. Those around me were shaken by the jury's call for the death penalty for me."

Angie said she was pissed her attorney never let her explain to the jury what really happened to Frank. It wasn't murder she told the court room.

"There are no eyewitnesses and no poison found. Only a bush in my neighbor's yard. You have only speculation. I did point the finger at a child molester and hoped to expose him. I had so much on my head to handle by being homeless.

"When I saw Frank dead, I lost myself into the world of just existing. It does not equal murder. Yes, the cause of death was oleander and antifreeze. You must have determined how I got it into him. This is the essence of the charge. So the DA needed to prove the charge of murder by administration of poison was done by me."

Pounders cut in. He told Angie he was only going to allow her fifteen more minutes. The court had other business.

"I'm trying to show you this murder was not proven," she said. "These are things that needed to come out that didn't for three years. I can't show emotion. Everything that happened in that jail contributed to what happened."

Pounders cut her off again.

"This is argument and not evidence. You are saying your lawyer wouldn't let you testify. This is not going to change anything."

Angie went back to talking about Frank. She advanced her own theory about what happened.

"He was a special-education teacher. He was military. He was trained in poisons. He talked about poisons before the insurance. If he tells someone perhaps children are poisoning me, listen to him. There is no way I could give my husband more than sixteen to twenty-four ounces of thick, green antifreeze. The homework that you didn't do was oleander. Oleander numbs the mouth. His mental state was never brought up.

"My husband had mental problems. It's in the evidence. My husband had training with poison. That's in his background. I'm sorry for what I've done. All the lies.

Pointing the finger. I'm sorry I did that. When he died, I broke. I'm sorry."

Pounders said he was confused.

"Are you suggesting he took his own life?"

Angie took the bait. It was almost as if she was back talking to Joe Bob over coffee in her living room.

"You know what? I am. ... I don't have remorse. That's the evidence. I don't know how to show emotions."

And then, for the first time, Angie began to talk about Alicia's death. She was outside for a reason.

"I heard the paramedics coming. I was the only one there to do what has to be done. I was outside to find them because otherwise they would have to go to each unit. I didn't kill my daughter. If I was going to kill my daughter the track marks would have been different."

But why get $50,000 in insurance? Why cash the policy? Pounders had questions.

"The reason we got that much is that she was premature. She wouldn't be able to get insurance later on. That was solid," Angelina said. "The amount of the insurance is not the issue. I didn't even know it was still in effect when she died."

"If I wanted her dead, I would have done it when she had problems with her apnea. I put too much effort into that child. That child was a survivor. I didn't kill my daughter. I have peace about that. Lots of people have insurance on their kids. You put more on someone who has problems. My other daughter is still alive. Every one of my husbands, except for Frank, is still alive. I don't know how to show emotion. I can't."

Pounders finally had enough. He pronounced sentence.

"You shall be put to death within the walls of San Quentin in a manner prescribed by law."

Angie shook as Pounders continued. He told the deputies

to take her out and ship her off to Chowchilla, where California's death row for women is located.

Pounders said Angie had an "abandoned and malignant heart."

On the way back to the lock-up, Angie threatened to kill two of her guards in the jail. She would be shackled and placed in leg irons the next time she came out of her cell.

Juror No. 7 was in court. She spoke to a reporter about Angie and how the case turned out.

"She's getting what she deserves," the woman said. "The only thing that would have swayed me was her defense attorney. He didn't really speak much for her. He said she was a bad person and he didn't like her."

Epilogue

Unlike California of the early 1960s, administration of the death penalty takes decades. Most prisoners on death row will never die at the hands of an executioner.

Much of the case took place against the backdrop of world events, and as a result was little covered by the local media at the time.

Angie's prelim took place during the 9/11 attacks. Her trial took place at the same time California was in the throes of recalling Governor Gray Davis and electing actor Arnold Schwarzenegger to office.

Upon her sentencing in 2004, Angie became the fifteenth woman on California's death row and the first sentenced in the Schwarzenegger regime. At this writing a decade later, there are twenty women awaiting the death penalty in California.

Among California's women who are eligible for lethal injection are baby killers, spouse slayers, extortionists, and drug fiends. They range from sixty-two-year-old Maureen McDermott, who killed her boyfriend to collect on an insurance policy, to thirty-four-year-old Brooke Marie Rottiers.

In 2010, Rottiers robbed and killed two men by stuffing their underpants down their throats and then taping plastic bags over their heads. This woman has problems. Echoing Judge Pounders, a judge in Corona, California, described the act as a "cold, callous, brutal, and particularly cruel" crime.

In 2005, Angie sat for an interview with a reporter and refused to take any responsibility for Frank's slaying or the murder of Alicia.

The reporter recounted Angie's life and intimate details and noted that Angie was so lawsuit happy that just before she was arrested, she was preparing to sue her landlord in Montebello for asbestos poisoning.

Her sister said Angie "wanted the good life, but I also believe she felt the world owed her something."

Angie, who said she was high on pills and booze most of the time, maintained her innocence and blamed Frank for his own death.

"How could I get all that green goop into this intelligent man? I might have been depressed, I might have been sad, but I'm not an idiot."

By then she was cut off from her former friends and members of her family. Most, including her daughter, vowed never to speak to her again.

A decade after Pounders sentenced Angie to die, the California Supreme Court, in an eighty-eight-page published opinion, upheld the sentence in a single word: "Affirmed."

In a single word, the U.S. Supreme Court, led by Justice Anthony Kennedy, said Angie would have no chance to be heard at the federal level: "Denied."

She's out of court dates. But it remains unlikely she—or any other California inmate on death row—will be executed.

Located about halfway between San Francisco and Los Angeles, Chowchilla, formally known as the Central California Women's Facility, is the largest women's prison in the United States and one of the largest in the world. Built in 1990, the facility covers 640 acres in a region surrounded by almond trees, vineyards, and cattle ranches.

Besides death row, a wide variety of inmates, who might

be from the cast of *Orange is the New Black*, are held at the site including petty thieves, drug runners, disgraced politicians, and bank robbers.

There are those who say a story such as Angelina's is hard to tell and even harder to read because we become emotionally conflicted. It is easy to feel sorry for little Angie, the tragic preschool child who was raped by her grandfather. But once her body begins to change, although her adolescent physical grooming is years behind the manipulative emotional grooming by Grandpa, she is suddenly mocked by family members as the recalcitrant slut, the materialistic little bitch who used sex to manipulate and exploit others.

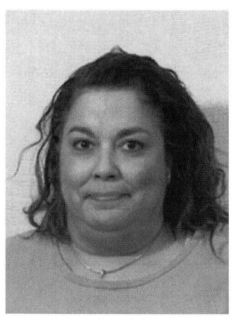

A stint on California's Death Row in Chowchilla has taken its toll on the once beautiful Angelina. Even though she has gained weight, she sometimes seeks out pen pals via Internet advertisments. (State of California)

Is that a surprise? Experts know that victims of molestation who experience incestuous relationships either become sexually frigid and adverse to physical intimacy or they become very sexually active and appear "promiscuous," but that is to misread their behavior.

In the past, they had no choice with whom they had sex. Now, however, it is their personal choice whether or not to have sex with someone. Each sexual act is re-affirmation of their individual right to choose their own sex partners.

There are heroes in this case. Certainly Deputy Brian Steinwand and Sgt. Joe Bob Holmes should be commended for their work. And, in fact, both were honored by their peers for cracking the case.

Steinwand, new to the homicide bureau when he caught the case, still describes the investigation as one of the best of his career.

"It was a once in a lifetime," he said. "She could have very easily kept her mouth shut, and she would have got paid off."

Angelina's best friend and "star witness" Palmira Gorham died suddenly, but not suspiciously, of cancer on August 23, 2004. Palmira's mother, Helen Morones, died in 2013.

The world hasn't completely passed Angelina by. Inmates on death row have access to TV, DVD players, computers, and the internet.

Harvest Time International Network, a Christian Ministry based in Laguna Woods, California, runs an outreach ministry which targets female inmates on death row at Chowchilla. Angie, a regular participant, leads Bible study once a week. McDermott and Rottiers take part in the same classes. How inspirational.

The once hot little number from the projects looms large on death row. Her size has increased dramatically since her arrest. In essence, she's gone from "juvenile jail bait" in her grandpa's bed to the Jabba the Hut in maximum security.

Death row is far more sterile than Twin Towers. Unlike Twin Towers, there's even a Yelp review or two. One review, done by a woman who identifies herself as a former employee, gives the facility two stars.

"Work is so stressful, management is not good plain and simple. I only had one opportunity to go in the prison and it didn't look too bad except when you walk into the medical portion of the prison. There were inmates yelling at workers, workers yelling at inmates. What a mess."

To stave off loneliness Angie posted a profile on WriteAPrisoner.com. It's wedged between the profiles of a Jose Rodriguez, who "spends a lot of time in the law library and drawing for my nieces, nephew, and godchild," and that of Samantha Rodman.

In 2006, Rodman, an El Paso teen, covered her face with a stocking mask then used a kitchen knife to stab her mother to death. She is serving a life sentence. She writes online: "I'm very reserved, but once I allow myself to open up then it's full on Sam. That's the name I go by: Sam. I'm very considerate and attentive to any friend or partner I may have. I'm hoping to meet good friends to help me do my time."

Angie's profile is far less verbose, yet more to the point:
Hello!
I am seeking a pen friend who: has a great sense of humor and personality, who is compassionate and nonjudgmental in nature, is easy going in conversation and disposition; an all-around good person.
I am half Puerto Rican originally from New York. I enjoy various types of music and books, I adore animals, beautiful scenery and like learning about cultures, places and new things. If this sounds like

you, want to know more? I look forward to hearing from you soon.
Ciao for now.
No journalists welcome
"Angelina"

The would-be Kojak who killed her husband, allegedly murdered her own baby in order to sue Gerber, and desperately tried to kill her best friend is surprisingly judgmental.

She doesn't like journalists

Authors' Commentary

Who killed Angie's husband? The cops and court say Angie did it, and you won't get an argument from us on the proven motive, means, and opportunity. There are more factors at play in Angelina's personal history than most folks are comfortable contemplating, and the Wicked Widow of Montebello was most likely not Angelina, but Victoria.

Remember her? Probably not. Few do. She was mentioned in passing, but she is an entity whose existence is sadly stereotypical. Victoria is the girl who "replaced" Angie when Grandpa was having sex with Angie's body. Angie would leave, and it was Victoria who took over. It was Victoria who knew all the right moves, it was Victoria who, more out of eagerness to engage in the acts than any desire to protect Angie, shoved Angelina out of the way. Victoria knew how to make an old man happy. Victoria knew how to accomplish all sorts of things, and soft little Angie never minded letting Victoria fill her shoes or her panties.

Angie's sister made a comment regarding the episodes of incest with Granddad and that he stopped that behavior with the other kids "about the time when that sort of thing should stop."

Frank Girardot and I found it a strange statement. In fact, she knew what she was talking about. Incest relationships, such as the one she described, have a standard duration of no more than three years. Anything beyond that and you are moving into a different realm of incest, as Gigi noted when she asserted that her sister wanted to perpetuate it.

This is where people get uncomfortable; this is where that which people think they know conflicts with what is known by those who study and research a specific topic. What screws kids up the most in incestuous families isn't the sex, it is all the other family factors that bring the incest aspect to public knowledge.

Consider: ninety percent of incest situations are never reported. Of the ten percent that do come to the attention of social services or law enforcement, it is *not* the incest that attracts their attention. Incest, after all, is secret.

What brings the attention and intervention is the overt and obvious, not the secretive and suppressed. Child Protective Services and/or law enforcement notice signs of neglect—continual bruises from daily abuse, thousands of disgusting parasites living, loving, and laying eggs in the child's hair, or the clusters of body lice living in the filth captured in unwashed body crevices.

Most pathologies arise from everything *other than* the incestuous sexual activity, and the sexual contact, despite being socially unacceptable and completely inappropriate, may be the only interaction in the kid's life that seems affectionate, nurturing, positive, and rewarding. While the sexual aspects are not understood by the child, and they may sense or discern that there's something "off" about it, they do know one thing for sure: they receive praise and validation from their abuser.

When we hear grandfather-granddaughter incest, or father-daughter incest, we think of some drunken sexually aggressive uncouth white male having his way with a sobbing, powerless victim. Stripped of childhood innocence, the traumatized kid will be shamefaced in adolescence and sexually dysfunctional in adulthood.

Possibly, but not likely.

Ninety percent of incest acts are not violent or coercive. They are initiated after a period of hugging, comforting, kissing, and tender stroking—all acts of nonsexual, inter-personal intimacy considered nurturing and normal in healthy households. The nonsexual loving contact is no different than precoital contact in a sexualized relationship. In the incest relationship, it is foreplay. Hence, for the child, there is no perceived difference between sexual and nonsexual contact. No touch that isn't erotic. As the affair continues, the child enjoys the extra attention, special treatment, gifts, and rewards. Read that sentence again, and let it sink in.

When little kids are rescued from these situations, they are (rightly) regarded as a "victim" of abuse. It is a tragic error, however, to assume the victim didn't find the experience pleasurable. Quite the contrary. They eventually discover that not only was the behavior "bad" but their response to it was also "bad" or "wrong."

If they enjoyed the physical sensations, they must never say so. If the sex was rough and wild, they will, as an adult, deny any affinity for rough and wild sex and say they seek a lover of tenderness and romance.

There's a story told to Frank by a homicide detective who knew a surviving male victim of a brutal serial rapist and killer who had trouble adjusting in adult life to the fact that he was stimulated during the rape.

Experts say that whatever you first experience sexually, you will replicate or reenact those early experiences the rest of your sexual life. Angie married Tom Fuller because he was everything she was "supposed" to want—handsome, healthy, tender, loving, kind, compassionate, and a good protective father. Obviously that couldn't last because what Angie really wanted sexually was adrenaline fueled, taboo interaction. When Tom left town, Angie got down.

As the victim matures—using Angie as an example—they learn that they were supposed to hate every minute of their "involuntary" sex life. They learn to lie, they learn to pretend, and they master the art of forever being victimized. They continually seek to "get even," complain constantly about their never-ending mistreatment and lack of respect to the point where no one respects them, and folks fantasize about mistreating them.

Except those who want to jump upon the victimization bandwagon.

"The reality of the victimization of children," wrote social psychologist Carol Tavris in "Beware the Incest-Survivor Machine," published in the *New York Times* on January 3, 1993, "is being obscured by a chorus of adults clamoring that they were victims too—if not as children, then as infants; if not in this life, then in a previous one. The evidence that abuse is more common than we knew is being trivialized by invalidated claims made by pop-psychology writers that abuse is nearly universal, and that if you can't actually remember the abuse, that's all the more evidence that it happened to you."

Angie had no trouble remembering her abuse, and neither did anyone else in the family. It is said that blame is only important to drunks and lawyers—often the same thing. Grandpa shoulders the blame for the misapplication of his genitalia, but the extended family shares culpability in the deadly aftershocks of Angie's childhood sexual exploitation.

The personality traits of those who have experienced incest, delineated by Michael H. Stone, MD in "Incest-Related Syndromes of Adult Psychopathology," include symptoms manifested most assuredly by Angelina.

Anger, irritability
Jealousy
Emotional volatility

Mistrust suspiciousness
Irresponsibility, disregard for social rules and customs
Manipulativeness, exploitativeness
Seductiveness
Deceitfulness
Secretiveness
Coyness [artfully or affectedly shy or reserved; slyly hesitant; coquettish]
Dependency
Hostility
Low self-esteem
Masochism
Shame

That's quite a list, but it is only the overture to characteristics manifested by Angie.

Depression, suicidal preoccupation, and behavior
Rage outbursts, substance abuse, antisocial behavior
Anxiety, fearfulness
Dissociative tendencies/multiple personality disorder
Ambivalence, with a tendency to oscillate between adoration and vilification

Look at Angie's choice of lovers. She marries a kind-hearted handsome man with good hygiene, healthy habits, and plenty of love in his heart—so she runs off to get her brains banged out by a fellow speed freak in a low-rent rendezvous. And Angie does this more than once—it becomes a pattern. It is like a twist on the old maxim, "There is the girl you marry, and then there is the girl who is your mistress."

For Angie, there were those men that society's "script" said she should marry, and then there were the men she lusted after. They were not the same guys.

Let's get back to Victoria—the secondary personality wandering around in the consciousness of Angelina. Okay, it is a stereotype, but that's because the formation of secondary personalities by victims of incest is stereotypical.

Psychologists and psychiatrists continue to wrestle with the reality of what used to be called Multiple Personality Disorder, now termed Dissociative Personality Disorder. Just for the sake of discussion, let's say that overtime Angie gets stable, gets a good husband, and attempts living a "normal life." Victoria gets aggravated. That isn't what she wants, and she knows what to do about it.

And yet, we come to the bottom line—Angie killed Frank dead. She keeps making up stories—first she blamed it on someone else, then she claimed Frank did it to himself. Nope. It was Angie or Victoria, and they have the same physical address.

At sentencing, when Angie addressed the court, she didn't speak a word about the loss of her beloved husband, Frank, or tearfully insist that this was all a tragic error. No, she complained of her treatment in jail.

Just as gravity pulls all things to the center of the earth, an exclusive love of self pulls all things to the center of the individual's universe—their own self, their own needs and desires.

Perhaps there are those in Frank's church who would say that she was possessed by Satan—the devil made her do these horrid acts. Research into origins of theological concepts belies the reality of any such *good god/bad god* dualism.

It is easy to call Angie evil. Once we call someone evil we don't have to deal with the fact that they are a real person, a human being who was once someone's darling little baby. Each child is potentially the light of the world. Angie's light was dimmed and distorted by that which she experienced in her formative years. That isn't an excuse. Not at all. It is simply an acknowledgment that Angie was forever damaged in shipping and handling, and some of her contents settled in a most unfortunate manner.

Punishment, be it forever in prison or six feet under, is not going to alter Angie's mental makeup or behavioral patterns—if she's dead she can't kill anyone else, that's for sure. The value of Angie being in the penitentiary is not that she will become penitent, but that we will be protected.

Angie is not "normal."

What is "normal"? Normal is what you are familiar with, what you are used to. Angelina is much like a confused cork in a tempest tossed ocean. Should she arrive safely on dry land, she would long for the familiar turmoil of the sea storm.

There is not much to say about Frank Rodriquez. He was one hell of a good guy, and she killed him for money. What can we learn from this? Well, that depends on how honest and perceptive we are willing to become.

When asked if there were a moral to the movie *Titanic*, someone replied, "Yes, never trust an old woman with expensive jewelry."

The moral of Angie's story is that sexual abuse of children, even when the abuse is nonviolent and rewarded with gifts and praise, leaves lasting emotional scars manifested later in life by behavioral symptoms that can include a callous disregard for the well-being of others, even to the point of calculated, cold-blooded murder.

Included herein are contacts and resources for those of you reading who are dealing with issues related to incest or other forms of sexual abuse. Yes, you may be embarrassed that such a "bad thing" may have also felt good. Sex is supposed to feel good, but the fact that it felt good doesn't make you bad or to blame for the inappropriate behavior of someone else. And from what we know of incest, it is multi-generational. The abuser was most likely also abused. An incest survivor recently shared online about her abuser: *He was molested as a child, far worse than I ever was. I do not offer that as any type of justification; it just helps me make sense of it all.*

This chain of shame doesn't end until the abuse is overcome, compassion increases, and we cease blaming the victims for not fitting the pattern of our expectations.

One final comment for those of you new to the true crime genre. Authors such as we do not reap great wealth from writing these books, and there is no contemporary genre as maligned as "True Crime."

Consider this: no one sends letters to newspapers calling them nasty names for writing stories about crime, despite many newspapers' unabashed willingness to sensationalize stories to increase circulation. After all, newspapers are for-profit businesses, not public-service entities.

Television, with the exception of viewer-supported programming on public television, is also about ratings and income. Even television "news" is no longer under a separate "News Division" at the networks. It is classified as "Entertainment."

Television and radio talk shows may devote an hour to an in-depth analysis of a particular homicide or series of homicides. No one complains that they are bloodsuckers.

And yet, when dedicated investigative journalists devote a year of their lives and their own personal resources to fully examine and bring to light the details of a case that a newspaper doesn't have room to explore and television doesn't have time to cover in full, they are accused of profiting off the pain of others.

This breaks our hearts.

True crime authors such as Frank C. Girardot, Jr. and I write these books in the hope that the lessons learned will save lives. Our goal is to raise the victim's death to the level of sacrifice. If this book saves someone from a life-long trauma of incest or abuse or keeps someone alive who otherwise might have been murdered, then Frank Rodriguez did not die in vain.

As for the allegation that Angie murdered her own toddler daughter—an allegation she continues to deny, and one that her sister also does not think could possibly be true—we would appreciate your personal opinion. Please send us an email letting us know what you think.

Burl Barer & Frank C. Girardot, Jr.
Wild Blue Press
January 2016

Abuse Survivor Resources

ASCA (Adult Survivors of Child Abuse) by the Morris Center

The organization offers support resources designed specifically for adult survivors of physical, sexual, and/or emotional child abuse or neglect. Support groups are available in the USA, Australia, South Africa, and on the web.

Website: www.ascasupport.org

Address: The Morris Center, P.O. Box 14477, San Francisco, CA 94114

Domestic Violence Survival

The online guide provides information and referrals to shelters, crisis, long, and short-term counseling, legal assistance, and document and lock replacement.

Website: www.domesticviolence.com

National hotline: 800-799-SAFE (7233)

New York hotline: 800-621-HOPE (4673)

Gift From Within (GFW)

The site is dedicated to those who suffer post-traumatic stress disorder (PTSD), those at risk for PTSD, and those who care for traumatized individuals. It provides articles, book reviews, coping ideas, poetry, and peer support through the pal network for women suffering from PTSD.

Website: www.giftfromwithin.org

Address: 16 Cobb Hill Road, Camden, ME 04843

Phone: 207-236-8858

Fax: (207)-236-2818

Incest Survivors Anonymous (ISA)

The organization offers self-help/mutual-help twelve-step support groups for survivors. Write or call for groups and meeting information and literature—specify you are a survivor.

Website: www.lafn.org/medical/isa/home.html

Address: P.O. Box 17245, Long Beach, CA 90807-7245

Phone: 562-428-5599

Office for Victims of Crimes

A justice-based site with resources, information, and assistance links for crime victims, including domestic abuse, child abuse, elder abuse, sex-trafficking, rape, and sexual assault.

Website: www.ovc.gov/help/index.html

Address: P.O. Box 6000, Rockville, MD 20850-6000

Phone: 800-627-6872

Fax: 301-251-5212

Pandora's Project

This site provides support and resources for survivors of rape and sexual abuse. Included are articles and resources as well as a support forum and chat area. It is one of the few forum sites open to minor survivors, ages 16 and older.

Website: www.pandys.org

Address: 3109 W. 50th St., Suite 320, Minneapolis, MN 55410

Email: admin@pandys.org

Phone: 612-234-4204

RAINN (Rape Abuse Incest National Network)

The network operates the U.S. National Sexual Assault Hotline and also provides a twenty-four-hour live secure online hotline for victims, friends, and family. It offers support and information about individual/group counseling, medical attention, reporting a crime, finding shelter, and many other services.

Website: www.rainn.org

Address: 2000 L St. NW, Suite 406, Washington, DC 20036

Phone hotline: 800-656-HOPE (4673)

Online hotline: ohl.rainn.org/online/

Safe Horizon

The organization provides resources for domestic violence, rape, sexual assault, and incest victims. The New York area programs include services for domestic violence, rape, sexual assault, child abuse, stalking, human trafficking, and homeless youths.

Website: www.safehorizon.org

Address: 2 Lafayette St., New York, NY 10007

Phone: 212-577-7700

Fax: 212-385-0331

The Sex Abuse Treatment Center

The organization helps female and male adults, teenagers, and children.

Website: www.satchawaii.org

Address: 55 Merchant Street, 22nd Floor, Honolulu, HI 96813

Hotline: 808-524-7273

The Sexual Assault Crisis Center

Programs include state-wide Spanish and English twenty-four-hour hotlines, individual short-term counseling, support groups, advocacy, and benefit assistance.

Website: thecenter-ct.org

Address: 1 Dock St., Suite 320, Stamford , CT 06902

English Hotline: 888-999-5545

Spanish Hotline: 888-568-8332

Sidran Institute

This site specializing on PTSD and dissociation provides information, resources, media, articles, therapist listings, and educational information for survivors and their loved ones. In addition, they offer educational resources to professionals, students, and the media.

Website: www.sidran.org

Address: P.O. Box 436, Brooklandville, MD 21022-0436

Phone: 410-825-8888

Fax: 410-560-0134

SocialWorkDegree.net

The online guide provides a list of over 100 organizations throughout the US that offer counseling, advice, and even shelter to members of families where domestic violence has occurred. The sources listed include: advocates for better policies and social support systems, twenty-four-hour hotlines and crisis counselors, and organizations that support and help domestic violence victims in their healing and recovery psychologically.

Website: www.socialworkdegree.net/domestic-violence-prevention

Survivors of Incest Anonymous (SIA)

This organization offers a self-help, twelve-step recovery program for adult survivors of child sexual abuse. It defines incest and child abuse broadly and provides general information, as well as information on how to start a new support group.

Website: www.siawso.org

Address : World Service Office, P.O. Box 190, Benson, MD 21018-9998

Phone: 410-893-3322

Survivors Network of those Abused by Priests (SNAP)

SNAP provides support and knowledge to all victims of clergy abuse and advocates helping ensure that in future generations, children will be safe.

Website: www.snapnetwork.org

Address: P.O. Box 6416, Chicago, IL 60680-6416

Phone: 312-455-1499 or 877-762-7432

Survivorship

This site provides resources, healing, and community for survivors of ritual abuse; training and education for professionals who may serve RA survivors; and support for survivors' partners and other allies.

Website: www.survivorship.org

Take Back The Night (TBTN)

This foundation serves to create safe communities and respectful relationships through awareness events and initiatives.

Website: takebackthenight.org.

Email: An automated email contact form is available on the website.

Phone: 888-995-1113

Women Organized Against Rape (WOAR)

This organization provides crisis intervention services to help survivors who have recently been sexually assaulted. They also provide counseling and advocacy for survivors of sexual assault and sexual abuse, community education, and public information about sexual violence.

Website: www.woar.org

Address: One Penn Center, 1617 JFK Blvd., Suite 1100, Philadelphia, PA 19103

Hotline: 215-985-3333

Phone: 215-985-3315

Fax: 215-985-9111

YWCA Silicon Valley Rape Crisis Center

The organization's area programs include a twenty-four-hour crisis line for survivors, family members, and friends, accompaniment of survivors to the hospital and through the reporting and judicial process, peer support groups, child abuse and assault prevention programs, and free confidential crisis counseling.

Website: www.ywca-sv.org/donate/rape_crisis.php

Address: 375 South Third St., San Jose, CA 95112

Domestic Violence Crisis Line: 800-572-2782

Rape Crisis Hotlines: 408-287-3000 and 650-493-7273

Use this link to sign up for advance notice
of new books from Burl Barer and Frank C. Girardot Jr:
http://wildbluepress.com/AdvanceNotice

Word-of-mouth is critical to an author's long-term success.
If you appreciated this book please leave a review on the
Amazon sales page:
http://wbp.bz/atfmreviews

Coming Soon to WildBlue Press
The Trail of Ted Bundy
Digging Up the Back Stories

http://wbp.bz/thetrailoftedbundy
www.WildBluePress.com

THE TRAIL OF TED BUNDY

BY

KEVIN SULLIVAN

Within the pages of The Trail of Ted Bundy: Digging Up the Back Stories, you'll hear the voices - many for the first time - of some of Ted Bundy's friends, as they bring to light the secrets of what is was like to know him while he was actively involved in murder . The stories of his victims are here as well, as told by their friends, including the occasional bits of information that didn't make it into the investigative files and are being published here for the first time. Two of the former detectives who worked with me during the writing of The Bundy Murders, return to aid readers in fully understanding Bundy's murderous career; and in one instance, dispelling a commonly held myth pertaining to one of the murders.

Read More About The Trail of Ted Bundy At:
http://wbp.bz/thetrailoftedbundy
www.WildBluePress.com

COMING SOON TO WILDBLUE PRESS
ICE AND BONE
Tracking An Alaskan Serial Killer

ICE AND BONE: Tracking an Alaskan Serial Killer
by MONTE FRANCIS

In the Fall of 2000, in Anchorage, Alaska, a series of murders captured headlines, stoking fears a serial killer was on the loose. Six women, mostly Alaska Natives, were found slain, all under similar circumstances. An anonymous tip led investigators to a thuggish, young drug dealer, who would eventually implicate himself in three of the women's deaths. But it wasn't until the disappearance of a well-loved nurse psychologist seven years later, and the discovery of her body in the remote wilderness of Wasilla, that two astute female detectives would finally bring the murderer to justice.

ICE AND BONE is the chilling, true account of how a notorious murderer evaded police and avoided conviction only to slip back into the shadows and kill again. Award-winning journalist Monte Francis tells the harrowing story of detectives' hunt for a serial killer, recounting a case that sparked cries of outrage and racial injustice, and reveals why the true scope the killer's savagery is only now, more than a decade later, coming into view.

Read More About ICE AND BONE At:
http://wbp.bz/iceandbone
www.WildBluePress.com

**More True Crime You'll Love
From WildBlue Press.**

Learn more at: http://wbp.bz/tc

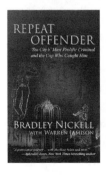  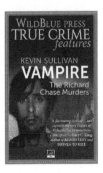

www.WildBluePress.com

More Mysteries/Thrillers You'll Love From WildBlue Press.

Learn more at: http://wbp.bz/cf

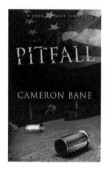
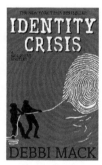
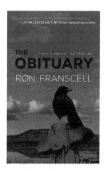

www.WildBluePress.com

Go to WildBluePress.com to sign up for our newsletter!

By subscribing to our newsletter you'll get *advance notice* of all new releases as well as notifications of all special offers. And you'll be registered for our monthly chance to win a **FREE collection of our eBooks and/or audio books** to some lucky fan who has posted an honest review of our one of our books/eBooks/audio books on Amazon, Itunes and GoodReads.

**Let Someone Else Do The Reading.
Enjoy One Of Our Audiobooks**

Learn more at: http://wbp.bz/audio

**Please feel free to check out more True CRIME books
by our friends at**

www.RJPARKERPUBLISHING.com

  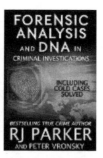